W9-BIB-489

NEW DESIGNS IN RAISED EMBROIDERY

NEW DESIGNS IN RAISED EMBROIDERY

BARBARA AND ROY HIRST

WE DEDICATE THIS BOOK TO THE
MANY EMBROIDERERS AND NEEDLELACE MAKERS
WHO HAVE PARTICIPATED SO ENTHUSIASTICALLY IN THIS
LATE 20TH-CENTURY STUMPWORK REVIVAL

First published 1997 by Merehurst Limited,
Ferry House, 51-57 Lacy Road, London, SW15 1PR

Copyright © 1997 Merehurst Limited

ISBN 1 85391 578 5

All rights reserved. No part of this publication may be reproduced, stored in a retrieval system, or transmitted, in any form or by any means, electronic, mechanical, photocopying, recording or otherwise, without the prior written permission of the copyright owner.

A catalogue record for this book is available from the British Library.

Edited by Diana Lodge
Designed by Bill Mason
Photography by Stewart Grant, except for pages 6–9, 25, 30, 60 and 61

Colour separation by Chroma Graphics
Printed in Hong Kong by Wing King Tong

CONTENTS

INTRODUCTION

Although the primary aim of this book is to encourage embroiderers to take up their needles, threads, fabrics, and dyes to create a personal piece of stumpwork embroidery, it is worth pausing to take a glance at the origins of stumpwork and at the domestic raised embroidery created by the aristocratic girls and ladies of 17th-century England.

Unlike painters, who normally make a practice of signing their work, these domestic embroiderers left almost no trace of their identity or where they might have lived. Despite the already overcrowded nature of stumpwork design, a considerable number of them managed to squeeze their initials, as well as a date, into the embroidery, but we are left to decide whether the date marks a special commemorative event or simply the year when the embroidery was worked.

In just a few tantalizing examples, a 17th century-embroidery reveals a little more about the embroiderer. The silver hasp and lock on the Sudbury Hall stumpwork box is engraved 'Hannah Trapham 1671'; a reframed panel at Hanley has attached information stating that it was worked by Miss Toombs of Luton who was at the court of Queen Anne; a panel in the Shelburne Museum (USA) bears the name Lydia Woolcott; there is good reason to believe that 'The Drowning of the Pharoh in the Red Sea', now in the Lady Lever Collection, was worked by Damaris Pearse when she was 16 years old, and of course there is Hannah Smith, who tells us that she went to live in Oxford in 1654 at the age of 12 and while there for two years completed the embroideries for a 'cabinete', now in the Whitworth Art Gallery, Manchester.

There are no strong links with a particular person in the case of the 'AYMEZ LOYAULTE' panel, seen here, but it is unlikely that anyone other than a family member would have had a sufficiently strong desire to display the family motto so

Aymez loyaulte *is the family motto of the Paulet family and the above embroidery, perhaps dating from c.1648-58, may have strong associations with John Paulet, fifth Marquis of Winchester, whose home, Basing House, was destroyed by Cromwell during the Civil War. The embroidery (ref. C1991.20) is a recent example of textile conservation by the Hampshire County Council Museums Service, Winchester, Hants.*

This well-preserved mirror frame owes its good condition to the leather-covered box in which it is housed. It is on display at Sulgrave Manor near Banbury, the home of George Washington's ancestors. Size: 43 x 35cm (17 x 14in)

This detail from the Tristram Quilt *depicts a ship bearing a banner emblazoned with fleur de lys and filled with rowing soldiers, and also a king-like figure on the poop deck blowing a boatswain's whistle and in a posture which suggests that he might be conducting or beating time. Courtesy of the Board of Trustees of the Victoria and Albert Museum, London.*

prominently, and we may never know who worked the unassembled panels for a box at Fenton House, Hampstead (see page 25), but the portrait which adorns the lid is said to be that of Elizabeth Coombe, one of the most celebrated needlewomen of the Stuart period.

In 1954 a fragile, but exquisite, stumpwork box bearing the initials EC in seed pearls, and dated 1678, was added to the stumpwork collection at the Victoria and Albert Museum, London. Remarkably rich in both techniques and the variety of stitches, the box is undeniably a virtuoso example of domestic stumpwork embroidery. An earlier owner, who considered it to be one of the finest stumpwork caskets in existence, describes the techniques as chain stitch, cross stitch, flat stitch, long stitch, tent stitch, tapestry stitch, needlelace stitch, chenil stitch, plush stitch, crochet stitch, crewel work, bobbin lace, Hungarian stitch, net work and bullion work, and in conclusion asserts that it is perhaps also the work of Elizabeth Coombe.

EARLY BEGINNINGS

The precise origins of raised embroidery (stumpwork) are lost in time, so one can only look back to a period when even earlier embroiderers were working in the narrative style. Using two layers of linen fabric, a cotton wadding sandwich, and white as well as light brown linen threads, Sicilian embroiderers created the narrative *Tristram* quilt in around 1400. In a series of fourteen scenes reminiscent of a strip cartoon, the quilt tells the story of the oppression of Cornwall by King Languis of Ireland, and the battle of Sir Tristram (or Tristan) on behalf of King Mark. Writing in the early 1920s, Theresa Macquoid suggests that this early pictorial quilting was perhaps the initial impetus to figurative stumpwork embroidery. This may well be so because within a half century professional Hungarian embroiderers were incorporating raised embroidery into their sumptuous ecclesiastical apparel, and in 1574-5 we would have found Wolfgang Popp busy in his German workshop creating *Das Salzschiff*, a guild shield which illustrates three figures in high relief about to land barrels of salt on the banks of the River Donan in the German town of Passau. Using wire, wax, wood, horse hair, metal threads and brocade-like fabrics, he was creating professional raised embroidery in the stumpwork style.

Concurrently, in Elizabethan England embroiderers were exploring the rich and exciting qualities of detached buttonhole stitch, which led to the 'flying' needlelace that adorns much Elizabethan embroidery.

By the 17th century, embroiderers living in the affluent environment of the upper classes, surrounded by woven tapestry, carved furniture, embossed plasterwork and silver, and influenced by a growing interest in science, plants, flowers, and all things religious and mythological, were seeking to interpret these in stitch. Although many embroiderers continued to create 'flatwork' embroideries in imitation of woven tapestry, others appear to have been influenced by the earlier raising techniques and the needlelace developed by the Elizabethans. Over a period lasting a few decades, these domestic embroiderers of Stuart England worked with remarkable industry and zeal to create a wealth of panels and boxes, caskets and bookcovers, as well as cushions and mirror frames, all in the raised embroidery style which the Victorians later renamed stumpwork. Although most of the large Victorian private collections are now dispersed, this has ensured that a larger body of people can enjoy this Stuart inheritance, either as owners or by visiting one of the many public collections around the world, and after more than three centuries stumpwork once again enjoys a growing popularity among embroiderers.

In this book, we include a range of projects in the 17th-century stumpwork style, starting with those which are comparatively simple and progressing gradually to advanced embroideries calling for skill and experience. It is our hope that, working in this progressive fashion, or using the projects and techniques as inspiration for personal design, users of this book will acquire the ability to design and create personal embroideries in this idiosyncratic style.

Wolfgang Popp's guild shield is one of several, all worked in a similar manner and, contrary to custom, secular in design. Courtesy of the Bavarian National Museum, Munich.

Worked by 'EC', this box is rich in stumpwork houses, castles, animals and flowers. Well-dressed ladies occupy the side panels, a squire and lady with their sheep decorate the front, and an elegant gentleman and his lady occupy the cartouche on the lid. Victoria and Albert Museum, London, photographed by Daniel McGrath. Size: 33 x 24 x 18cm (13 x 9½ x 7in)

CHAPTER ONE

STUMPWORK PANELS

Whether they are simple or sumptuous, 17th-century raised embroidery panels are comparatively small, and they only acquire their modest size by grouping together a disparate array of separate raised and embroidered motifs. The scale stems from the small size of each motif, together with the related use of fine thread techniques, and the character of stumpwork relies on both elements. Most of these panels were worked on an ivory or cream satin ground, much of which remains visible between the motifs. A small proportion, however, have a linen ground that is completely hidden beneath hand embroidery, which changes the character of stumpwork to a marked degree.

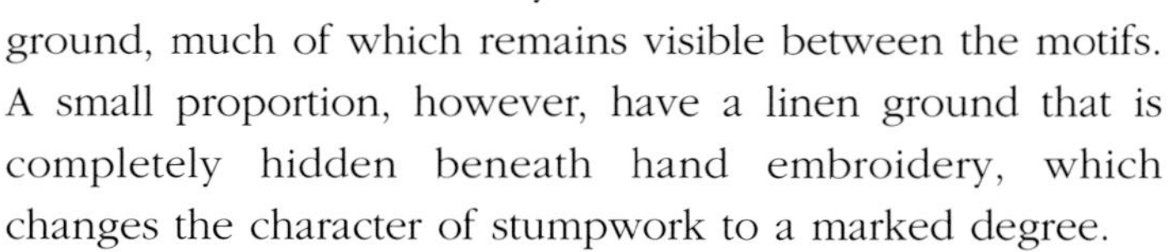

Sheep and the four seasons, in four small panels, is the combined theme for the first project. Each panel is smaller than its historical counterpart because it comprises only one motif and, being small, can be worked in a comparatively short time. The group of panels provides a range of stumpwork techniques as well as guidance on the preparation of the ground fabric and the final mounting and stretching.

For embroiderers who are interested in combining stumpwork with free machine embroidery, *Mr Brassica and Friend* and *Noah Plants a Vineyard* provide sign posts and are perhaps a natural progression to those 17th-century grounds that are completely covered in hand embroidery.

A medium-weight unbleached, and unwashed, calico (cotton) is the chosen ground fabric for all the projects in this book unless otherwise stated. The dressing in the unwashed calico serves as a natural resist during the wet-in-wet brush dyeing process. All creases must be removed from the ground fabric, with the aid of a damp cloth and hot iron, before any work commences. Use a light box when brush dyeing and transferring the design to the ground. Tape the fabric to the glass top of the box over the paper design; the light source will reveal the pattern, making it possible to transfer the design as described. Use a halogen lamp in the box to prevent the glass top overheating.

Sheep Shearer Two*, shows the shearer at work. Leather covers the padded sheep's head and body, and numerous embroidered slips in pendant couching create the fleece. Size: 18cm (7⅛in) square*

Evening Gold *combines free machine embroidery with raised figures and sheep in traditional 17th-century stumpwork style. The calico ground is richly dyed and the panel is edged with a gold-wrapped metal trim. Size: 20cm (7½in)*

STITCHES FOR SHEEP

The raised embroideries of the 17th century embraced a rich variety of hand stitches. If she knew a stitch, the embroiderer was likely to use it and also to innovate by mixing and intertwining it with others. We have this same freedom to use favourite stitches, add new ones, use a popular stitch in an unusual mode, or perhaps create a composite stitch which teasingly defies recognition. The stitches in this chapter have been chosen for these reasons and also because they provide imaginative sheep images. They can all be worked directly on the ground fabric to form background images, or on separate slips which will subsequently be applied to the main embroidery and, with the exception of tent stitch, perhaps raised with padding materials to achieve foreground effects in bold relief. Ordinary sewing needles or betweens will serve most purposes, but a fine ballpoint or tapestry needle is necessary for working the detached stitches. To retain the miniature scale, it is preferable to use threads no thicker than 100/3 silk.

French Knots

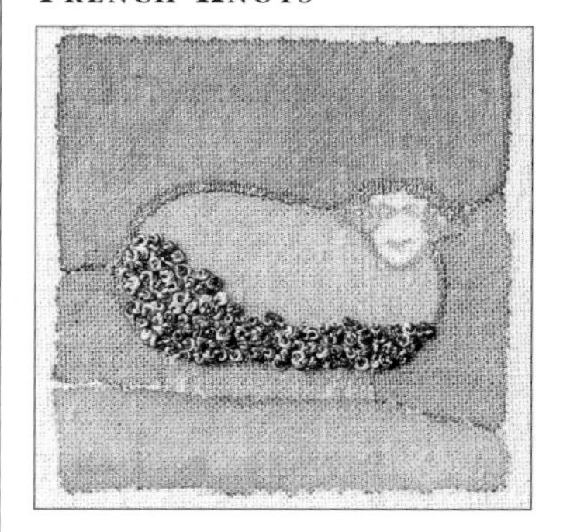

Two threads, differing in colour, are used in the needle in this example.

Pendant Couching

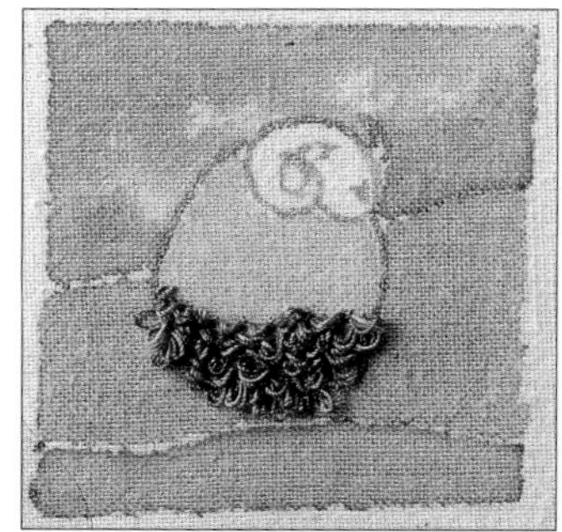

Groups of threads in several colours can be couched at the same time.

Bullion Knots

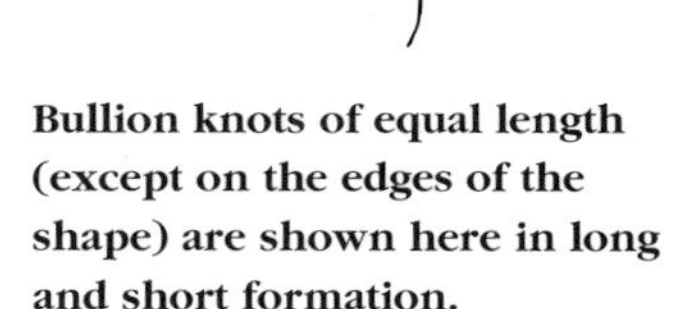

Bullion knots of equal length (except on the edges of the shape) are shown here in long and short formation.

Tent Stitch

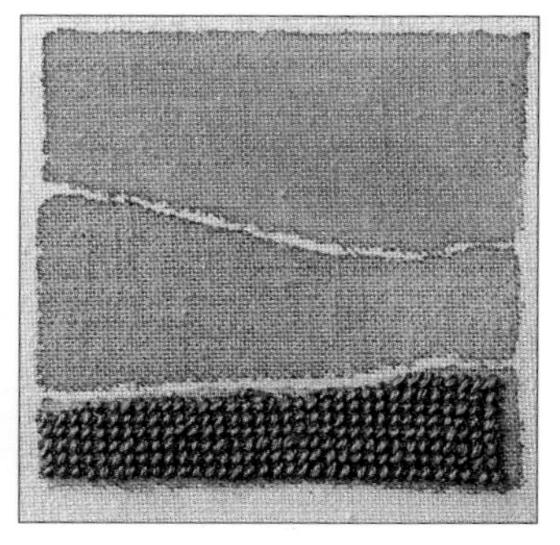

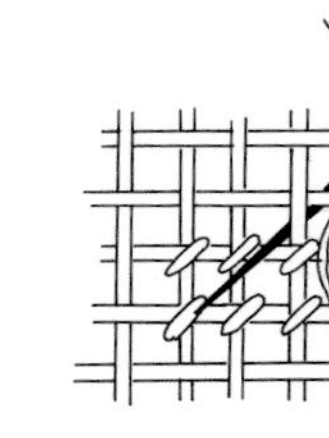

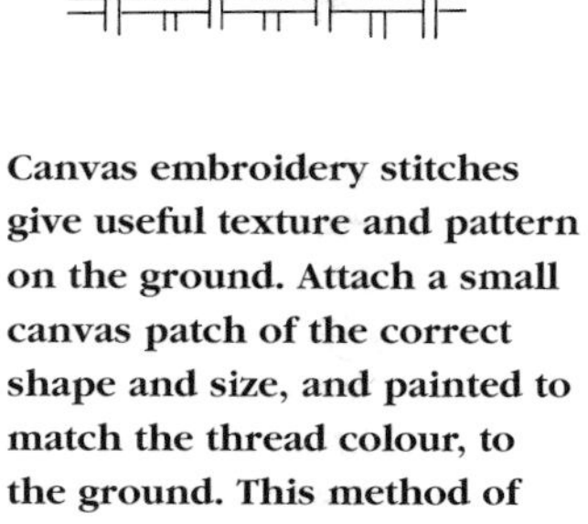

Canvas embroidery stitches give useful texture and pattern on the ground. Attach a small canvas patch of the correct shape and size, and painted to match the thread colour, to the ground. This method of working the canvas stitch through the canvas and ground (then usually satin) was used in the 17th century.

Spring Sheep is worked in French knots. Size: 15cm (6in) square

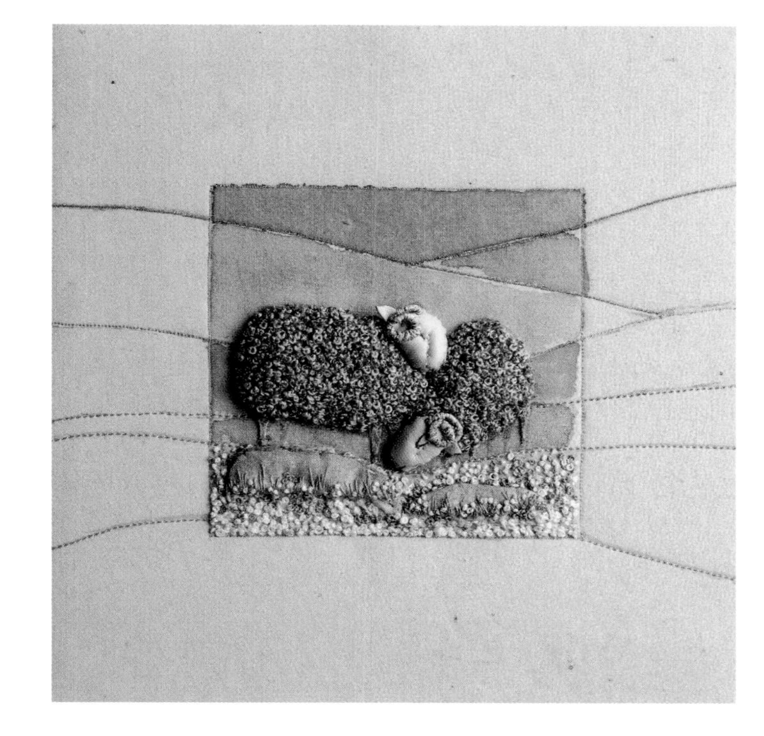

Suspended Buttonhole

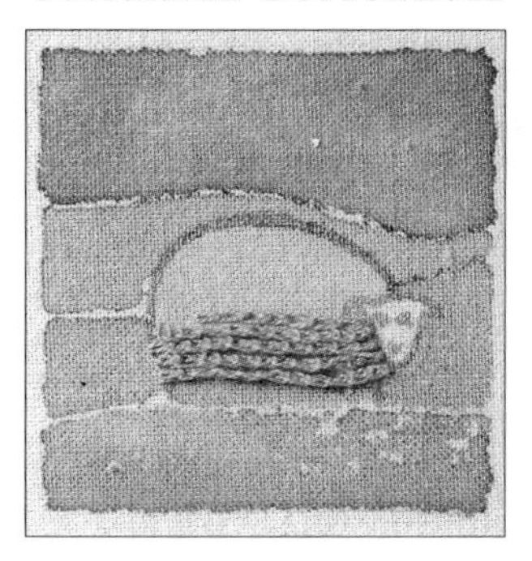

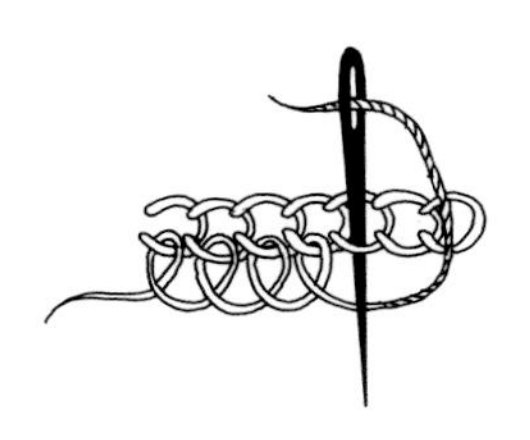

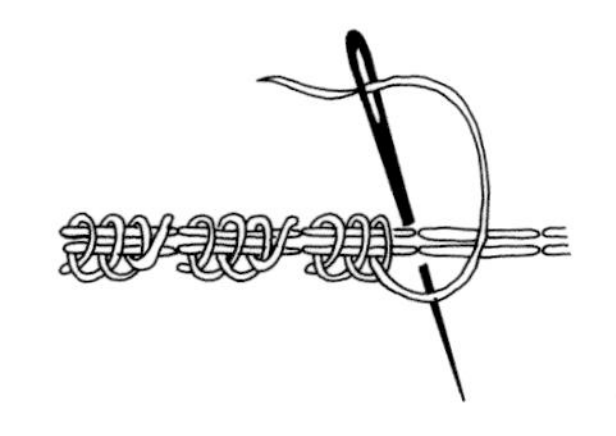

In this and the following example, buttonhole stitches are suspended from rows of other stitches. First, work rows of chain stitch then continue by suspending a detached buttonhole stitch from each chain stitch.

Alternatively, work two rows of back stitch close together. Working from the left, bring the needle through the ground below the first back stitch; fill the back stitch with detached buttonhole stitches, then take the thread through the ground above the back stitch to achieve an attractive twist to the group.

TRANSFERRING DESIGNS TO FABRIC

Summer Sheep is one of four small complementary panels. Enlarge the companion design drawing below until the outer square measures 15cm (6in). This is most easily achieved on a photocopier with enlarging facilities. Each panel features a simple design of folding hills, blocks of colour within an inner square, and coloured lines extending across a frame-like margin and continuing onto the edges of the panel. The edge design allows the finished embroidery to be stretched

Summer Sheep *features bullion knot bodies and a tent stitch foreground.*
Size: 7.5cm (3in) square (or 15cm/6in square if margins are added)

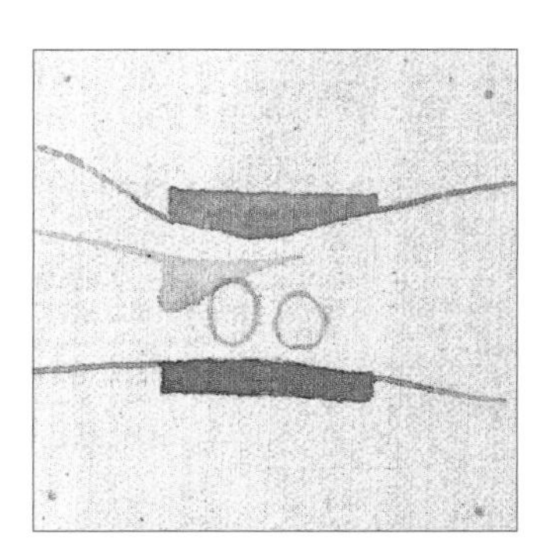

1 *Choose one or two separated shapes within the inner square and moisten (do not saturate) these shapes with water. Brush fabric dye/paint into the moist surface. Several colours can be allowed to coalesce in one area.* Paint all the coloured lines across the dry frame-like margins. When the dyes are dry, use gold fabric paint to outline the bodies of the sheep and mark the four outer corners of the panel. Temporarily remove the fabric from the light box to fix the dyes with a hot iron (or as instructed by the manufacturers).

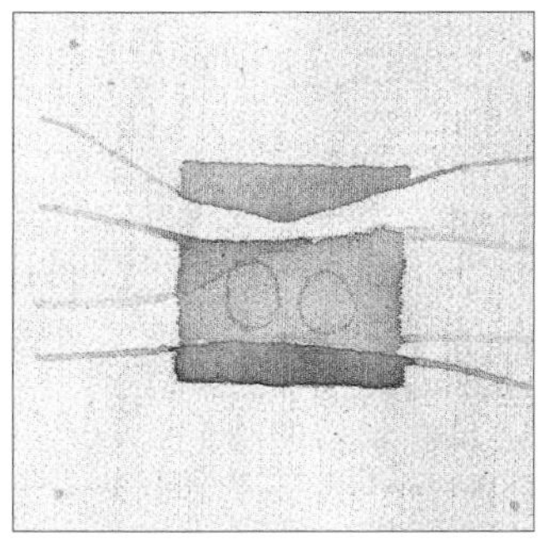

2 Choose further undyed shapes in the inner square and repeat step 1 from * to *. Remove the fabric from the light box and fix the dyes when the fabric is dry. Continue in this sequence until all the colours have been added to the inner square. Either dry calico or areas in which the dyes have been fixed must surround the shape which is being dyed. The colour will not trespass to any marked extent onto surrounding dry areas if there is sufficient dressing in the calico.

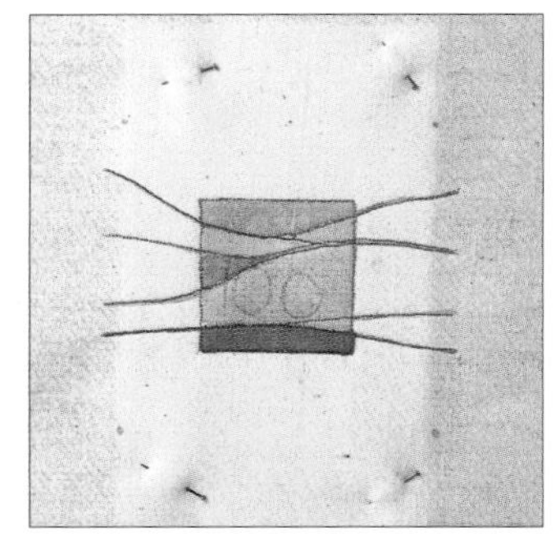

3 Cut a 15 x 23cm (6 x 9in) piece of white felt. Pin this beneath the ground fabric in line with the sides of the panel and keeping the pins beyond the top and bottom edges of the panel. Machine or hand quilt along the lines of the hills and around the edges of the inner square. Change the thread colours frequently to blend with the dyes. Pucker-free results will be achieved if the fabrics are stretched (machine embroidery style) in a round frame. Use a light box continuously for Steps 1 and 2.

over a 9mm-thick medium density fibreboard (MDF); it can be ignored if the embroidery is to be stretched over thin card.

Use gold fabric paint (or a mixture of white metallic pearl and ochre) to outline images and figures on the ground. This painted line, applied with a fine watercolour brush, always lies inside the edges of the same image on the design drawing, ensuring that it will not be visible on the finished embroidery.

The Scythers, *an idyllic scene from a past summer, uses matching calico fabric and threads for ground and covered mount, and silk dyes applied as described. Free machine embroidery on the ground and on organza slips sets the scene for the scythers, who are clad in traditional needlelace clothing. They swing scythes made from leather and silk-bound wires. Size: 20 x 24cm (7¾ x 9¼in)*

MAKING THREAD PURL

The 17th-century embroiderers decorated their raised work with metal purl which was either painted or silk-wrapped. A similar visual effect is achieved when silk or cotton threads are wrapped around a needle and coated in modestly diluted white glue. Allow sufficient drying time, do not over-dilute, and carefully follow the instructions below to achieve good results.

THREAD PURL

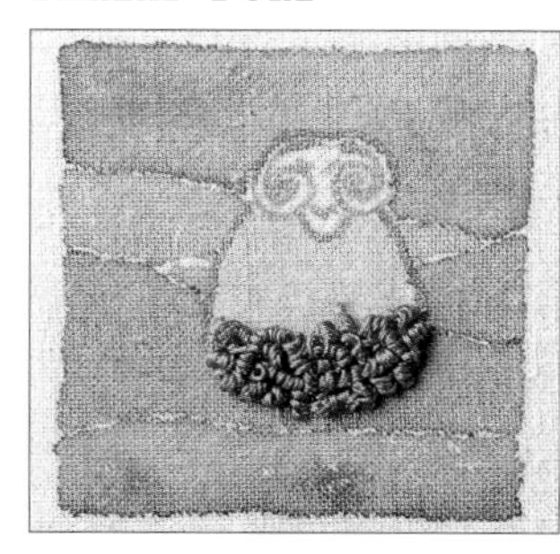

1 Closely wrap dry threads around the needle, near the point, and hold to prevent unravelling (12 or more wraps are possible). Using a watercolour brush, completely coat the wrapped threads with the glue. After about 20 seconds, push the threads fractionally towards the point of the needle to prevent sticking.

2 When the glue is set, remove the coil from the needle and cut the purl to any desired length. Using a separate thread, fix the purl lengths, like beads, through the core. Thread purl can be made and used in tightly wrapped coils (left) or in short coils with long dry tails (above) or in other modes for human hair.

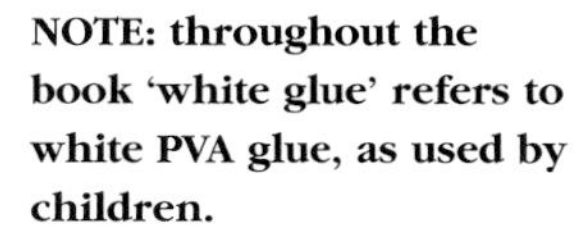

NOTE: throughout the book 'white glue' refers to white PVA glue, as used by children.

LEATHER HEADS AND EMBROIDERED SLIPS

These are made separately from the main embroidery on a lightweight calico ground on which the required shapes are outlined in gold fabric paint. The outlined shape for an embroidered slip will be slightly larger than that on the design drawing because the slip forms a pouch into which a soft filling is tightly packed. The outlined shape is painted to match the embroidery threads. Work with the fabric in a round embroidery frame (the kind which has an adjustment screw). Use fine needles and fine threads of matching colour when stitching leather to calico. Loose polyester (sometimes sold as Terylene or Dacron) is the ideal soft filling. Use the design drawing throughout.

The fleeces on Autumn Sheep *are worked in detached buttonhole stitches suspended on rows of back stitches and the machine embroidery in the foreground is worked on hard-edged slips. Size: 7.5cm (3in) square (or 15cm/6in square with added margins)*

Cutting and Stitching Leather

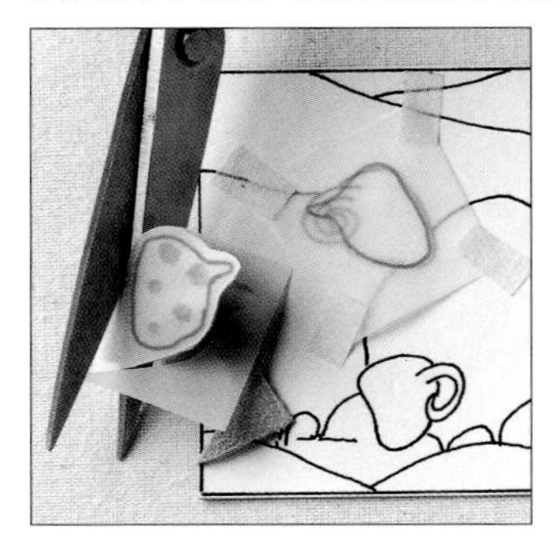

1 Make a tracing of the sheep's head; apply spots of white glue to the upper surface of the tracing paper within the head shape; attach a small piece of thin glove leather to the sticky surface. With small sharp scissors, and working from the reverse side, quickly cut out the head, leaving a generous margin beyond the traced outline and remove the tracing paper before it adheres permanently. Always use this method for cutting small leather shapes accurately.

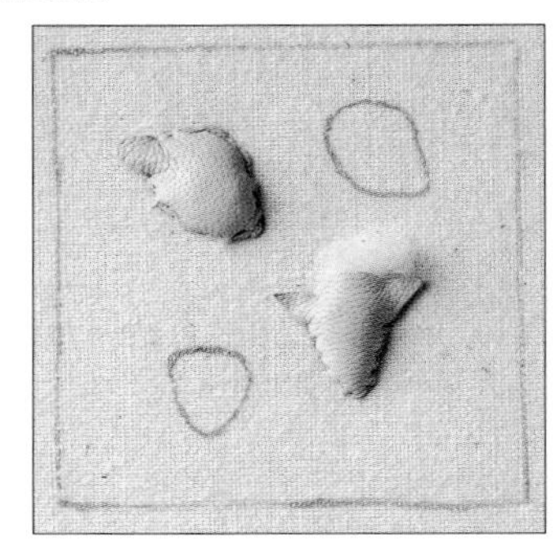

2 When attaching the leather to the lightweight calico, bring the needle up from beneath the ground on the outer edge of the gold line then return through the ground in almost the same position after stitching through the edge of the leather. Continue making these tiny stitches at equal intervals around the head. Tightly pack the shape with soft filling before completing the stitching.

3 For eyes and nose, work fly stitches (as shown in the diagram) through the leather head, adding back stitches in a matching colour to form the long bony nose. Two small stitches pucker the root of each ear, and French knots crown the head. Cut the head from the calico, leaving a 3mm (1/8in) allowance; run gathering stitches around the edge and draw the allowance under. The head will be attached to the embroidery in due course.

FLY STITCH

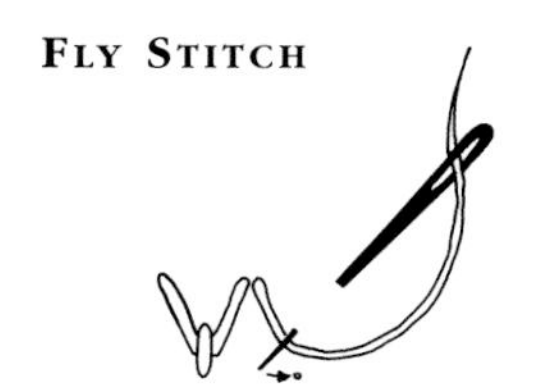

Winter Sheep *uses tightly-packed short lengths of thread purl for the fleece, a few straight stitches and bullion knots for fodder, and an applied flat machined slip for foreground snow. Size: 7.5cm (3in) square (or 15cm/6in square if margins are added)*

MAKING AND ATTACHING SOFT SLIPS

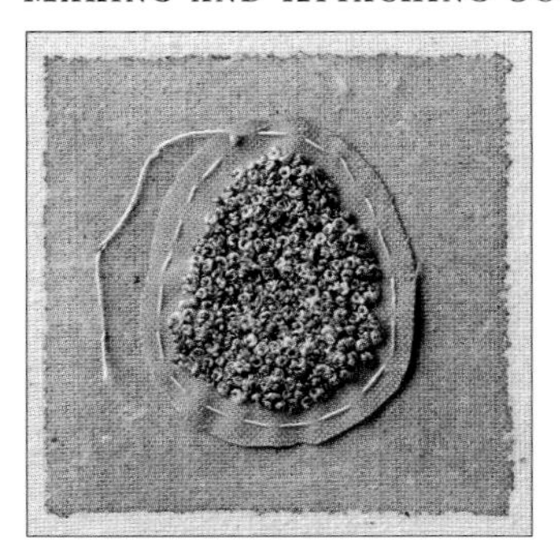

1 Fill the painted area within the gold outline with the chosen embroidery stitch (let the underlying dye, applied to match the thread colour, stray outside the gold outline to achieve a good edge finish to the applied slip). Leaving a 5mm/3/16 in allowance around the edge, run a line of gathering stitches around the edge, within the allowance, and cut out the completed embroidered shape. Draw in the gathering just enough to turn the edge under.

2 Attach the slip to the main embroidery with hidden stitches. Bring the needle up from beneath the ground on the outer edge of the gold line; return down again in the same place after catching the edge of the slip; insert sufficient soft filling for a good sculptural effect, but not beneath the head. Leather legs are stitched at the top and bottom to the main ground fabric; the top stitches are hidden by the slip while satin stitches, worked over the leather, fix the bottom and form the hooves.

MAKING HORNS

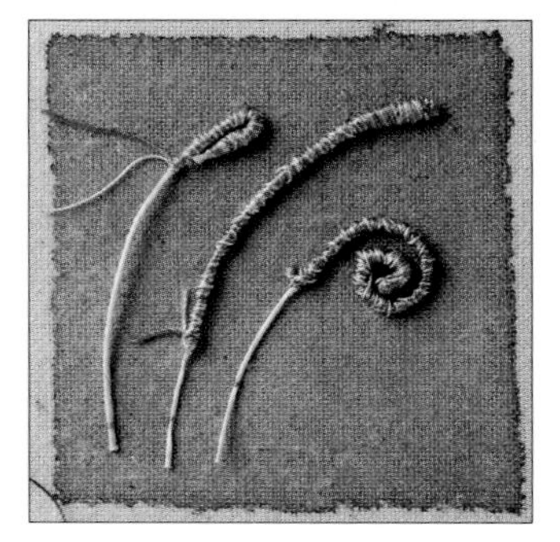

Having firmly stitched the head over the body with hidden stitches, the horns can be attached. To make a horn, either unevenly bind wire with masking tape and then wrap with thread, or simply bind the wire unevenly with thread. Leave some unwrapped wire at the root. Using a stiletto, puncture a hole through head, body, and ground at the appropriate point, insert the end with the bare wire, and bend and stitch it beneath the ground. It is also possible to attach the horns to the leather head before this is stitched to the main embroidery.

Hard-edged Slips

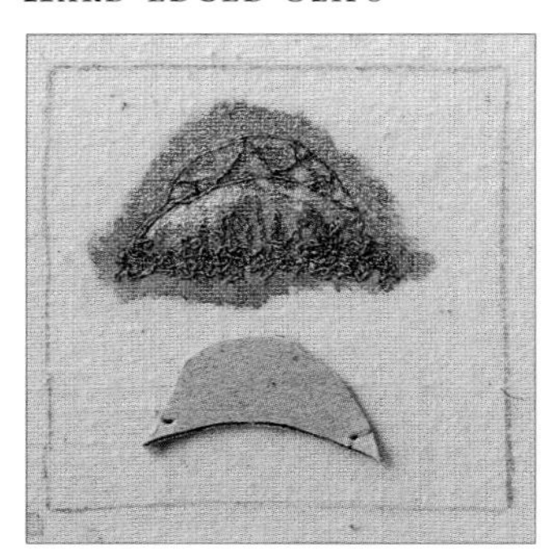

1 Transfer the required shape to the lightweight calico with gold or other outline; add dyes and/or acrylic colours as desired, followed by hand or machine stitching. Cut a matching card shape. Here, the lower edge of the embroidered slip blends in with the surrounding plants, so the lower edge of the card is cut away, but the fabric is carried down over it. In other cases, the slip will be fitted over the card shape at all edges.

2 Cut out the completed slip leaving a 5mm ($\frac{3}{16}$ in) allowance (perhaps a little more at the bottom). Snip around the upper edges as shown; stretch the embroidered slip over the card shape, and glue the upper edge allowance to the underside of the card with white glue. Insert soft filling between card and calico if a rounded, embossed effect is sought.

3 Attach the bottom of the slip to the main embroidery with hand or machine embroidery which blends with the surrounding work.

Frances Hawkens' distinctive raised embroideries show her interest in icons. The Lion Triptych, *which is inspired by a legend, incorporates stumpwork techniques including animal images formed as hard-edged slips. Size 28 x 18cm (11 x 7in)*

MOUNTING AND STRETCHING

If, as recommended, the embroidery has been worked in a frame, it will not be distorted, in which case you will have no difficulty mounting and stretching these small pictures. Stumpwork will suffer if it is placed face downwards, so work with the panel on its edge, or clamped edgewise between the knees. First line up the embroidery with the mounting board, which will have been cut accurately to size. Position the gold spots marking the corners of the embroidery with the corners of the mounting board and then proceed as described, using a strong button thread for the lacing. Use medium density fibreboard, or similar board materials, for thicker bases.

Mounting on Card

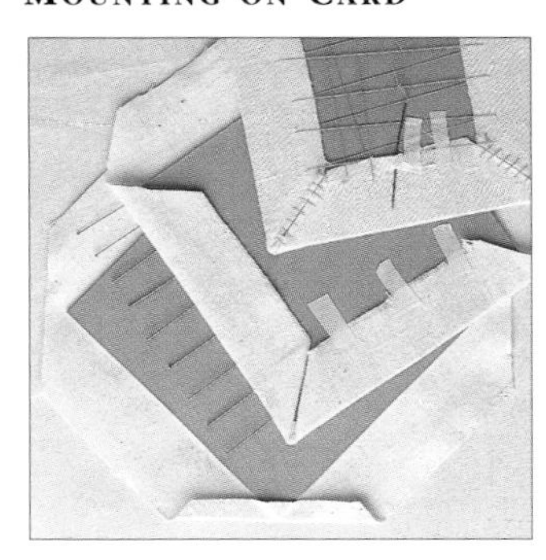

Trim the edges of the ground fabric, leaving sufficient for turning. Cut away the corners and fold the corner turnings (see lowest example). Fold over the turnings on opposite edges of the panel and temporarily edge-pin or tape in position (see middle example). Working across from one edge to the other, lace across the back and then, evenly, move to each thread in turn and stretch the threads taut before finally stitching or knotting off. Check frequently that the embroidery is correctly positioned on the mounting board.

Thicker Bases

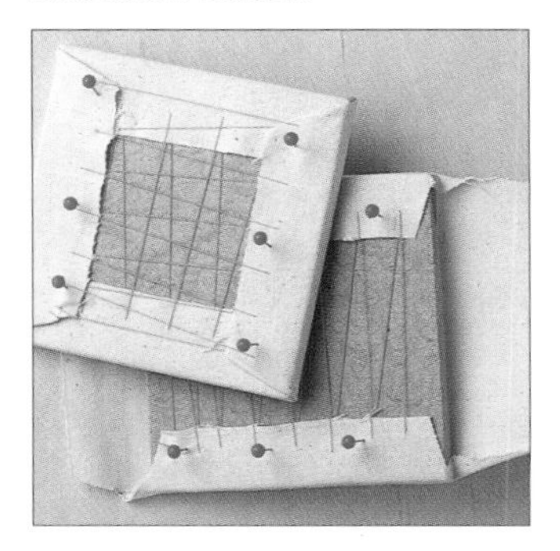

Proceed as already described, but cut and turn the corners as shown in the lower example. Drawing pins can now be used as a temporary fixing. Lace and stretch as already described. The corners can be stitched, but this is not usually necessary if the lacing threads extend almost to the edge of the panel.

Covering the Back

A piece of art card glued to the back of the panel can be decorative. The card sits better if the edges are scored and slightly bent. Paint the edge of the card to match the embroidery: run the brush along the edge, not up and down, which would deposit pigment on the back and front. Add title, date, embroiderer's name, and other information before covering the card with transparent self-adhesive film. Bond the card to the back of the embroidery with white glue. Weights (perhaps large books) on the edges of the face-up embroidery during the setting process will improve the finish. As an alternative, fabric can be ladder stitched to cover the back.

MACHINE-EMBROIDERED GROUNDS

The four sheep panels rely on small areas of texture surrounded by larger areas of dyed fabric ground. When the whole of a stumpwork ground is machine stitched, texture plays a dominant role and a balance must be maintained between the hand and machine textures. All the free machine stitching on the dyed ground should be completed before you add any stumpwork. When using a medium to heavy calico for the ground, in combination with fine threads, it will probably be necessary to use a No 90 machine needle (or thicker) for the free machine embroidery. Work in machine embroidery mode, with the fabric taut in a round embroidery frame; remove the foot (or use a darning foot) and render the feed dogs inoperative. The examples opposite include free running stitch (all machine dials set at 'O') as well as free zigzag and a free fancy stitch (using a chosen or variable stitch width). The visual and textural qualities will change when the embroiderer varies the machine speed, the pace of the fabric beneath the needle, or the tension settings. Using different threads for top and bobbin will also change the visual quality.

Mr Brassica and Friend *combines traditional stumpwork with overall free machine embroidery on a dyed calico ground. It incorporates larger-than-life cabbages freely machined on silk organza and assembled in the round. Traditional needlelace clothes the figures, which have soft sculptured calico heads and silk-bound wire hands and arms. Size: 20cm (8in) square*

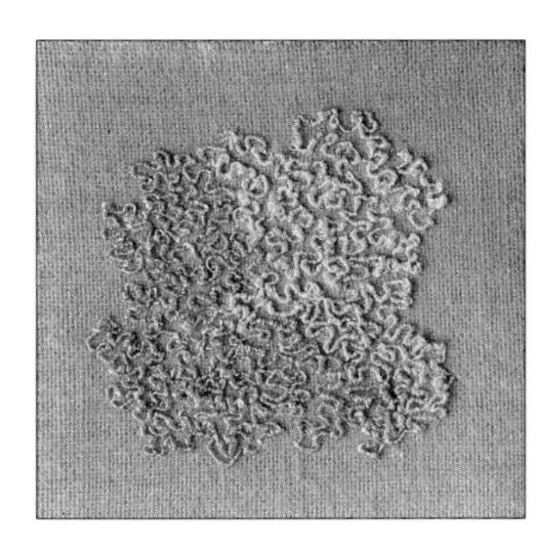

Vermicelli stitch is worked in a continuously reversing pattern of half circles. These can be small or large and the pattern can be tight or open.

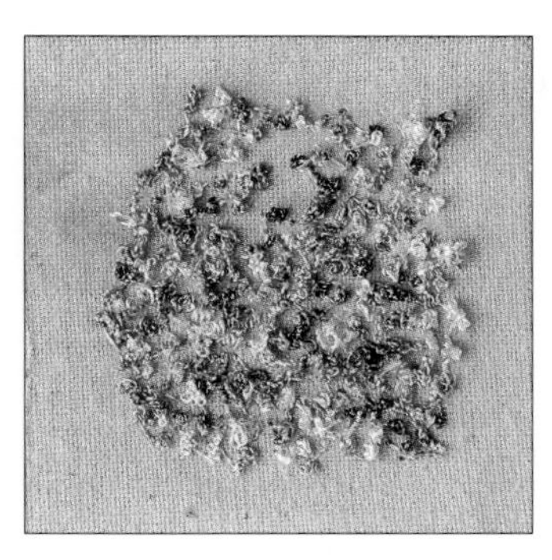

Make three or four stitches on the spot to produce a French knot effect. Move the fabric fractionally and repeat continuously.

Staccato backward and forward movements of the fabric produce a linear pattern with an irregular texture. The upper part of the example is overworked with vermicelli.

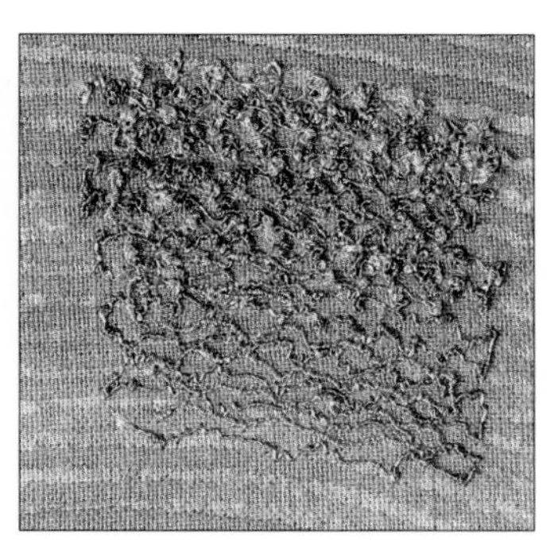

This free fancy stitch disintegrates progressively with each descending row as the fabric is moved at increasing speeds beneath the needle.

Double rows of free zigzag are separated here by narrow bands of straight running stitch.

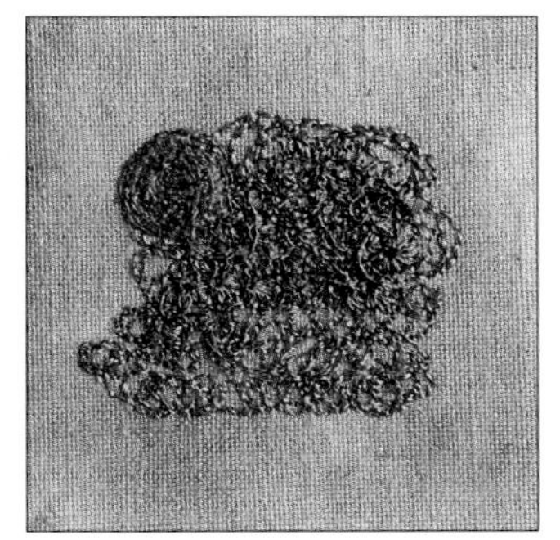

A constant circular motion is maintained in this example, which incorporates several layers of stitching, in different colours.

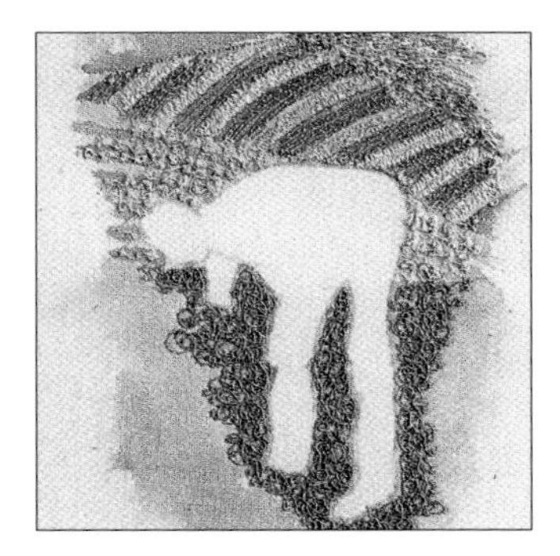

Stop the machine embroidery on the outer edge of gold design lines because these are needed to outline the shapes of the stumpwork. It is also very difficult to hand stitch through textured free machine embroidery with any degree of accuracy.

CONSTRUCTING FABRIC AND CARD MOUNTS

A machine-stitched mount of fabric and card is one method of creating a frame-like embroidered edge. Stretch-free fabrics work best, calico being used for the illustrated examples. The card is sandwiched between two layers of fabric. Before this takes place, the card is first cut to the size dictated by the embroidery, and any painting, dyeing, or machine embroidery on the top fabric is completed. Use the machine in normal stitching mode for Steps 2 and 5 and use white (PVA) glue for bonding.

1 Using white glue, bond the card to the bottom layer of fabric. Next, place the top fabric layer over the card and baste the fabric layers together, keeping the stitches tight against the outer edges of the card.

2 Machine a straight stitch tight against the four outer edges of the card then repeat around the inner edges. Next, work satin (close zigzag) stitch around the outer and inner edges; stitch around the edge repeatedly if desired and in a variety of different colours.

3 Working from the underside, trim away the bottom fabric, cutting tight against the satin-stitch edges and then cut away the upper fabric, leaving a 1cm (3/8 in) turning, and cutting across the outer and up to the inner corners.

4 Using either the flat surface of a table or a stout card, roll the 1cm (3/8 in) turning onto the back of the card and bond it in position. A spot of white glue on each corner will seal any raw edge.

5 Stretch the finished main embroidery in a round frame, in machine embroidery mode. Using extreme care, bond the finished card mount to the surface of the main embroidery. Now machine stitch the mount to the embroidery, using a straight stitch which follows the inner edge of the satin stitch.

A CONSTRUCTIONAL PANEL

Noah Plants a Vineyard is constructed from three separate embroideries, plus a ground to which they are attached. The stumpwork centre (a) is stretched over a card of irregular shape. Machine embroidery (b), which is worked in straight stitches and vermicelli, represents roof rafters and ceiling. When completed and stretched over its card mount, embroidery (a) was hand stitched to embroidery (b) and together they were then stretched and laced over a square of card. Embroidery (c) is a card and fabric mount which continues the roof rafter theme in straight and vermicelli stitches. All the embroideries were finally stitched to the dyed ground fabric (d), which was then stretched and laced over a thick base. The bold, sculptural design has a rich, medieval quality.

Noah Plants a Vineyard *was inspired by a wooden boss which sits high in the roof of Norwich Cathedral. Size: 16cm (6⅜in) square*

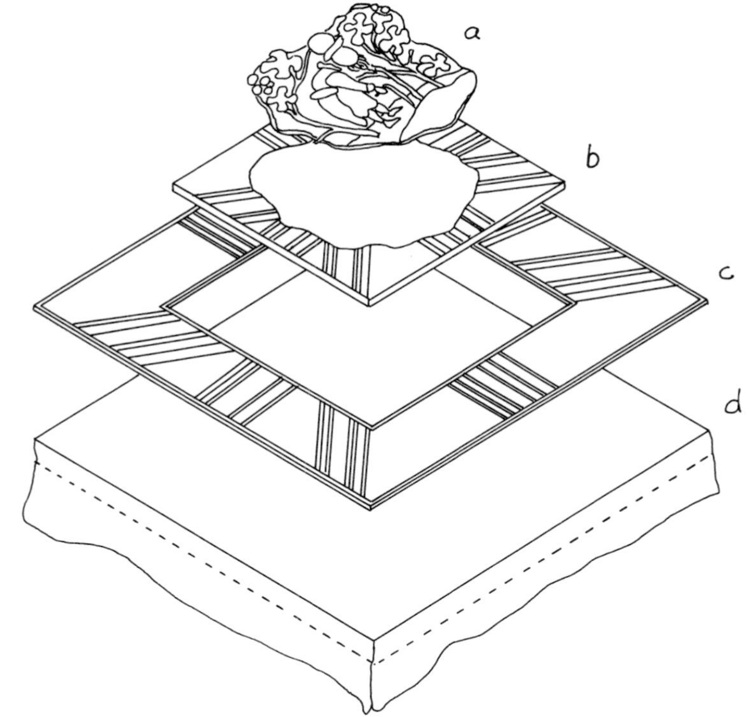

CHAPTER TWO

STUMPWORK MINIATURES

The creation of a really small raised embroidery in imitation of early painted miniatures is a unique and worthwhile project in its own right. Surprisingly, 17th-century domestic stumpwork enthusiasts ignored this genre, but miniatures of Charles I were embroidered in split stitch and padded satin stitch as late as about 1700. Charles I and II, of course, frequently feature on biblical stumpwork embroideries, usually standing in for Kings Soloman or David, but these are full figure portrayals rather than the miniature head-and-shoulders format.

Stumpwork likenesses are difficult to create, but facial shapes, hair styles, and strong characteristics, such as a beard or moustache, can all be conveyed with a combination of soft sculpture and thread techniques, and become the foundation for the contemporary miniature. After some practice, a soft sculptured stumpwork head can be successfully worked directly onto the ground fabric to exactly the correct shape and size. However, the same kind of head can be worked on a separate ground before being transferred to the main embroidery. This alternative method can prove useful for various reasons: if greater relief is required; if the head is being applied over other stitchery; when the head is in profile and consequently more difficult to form, or when the embroiderer has limited experience and might need more than one opportunity to create a well-formed head before stitching it to the embroidery.

The materials required are a well-washed lightweight calico (used on the cross grain), a loose polyester filling, natural coloured threads, and threads of the chosen colour for hair, together with a matching felt. White glue (one part) diluted with water (two parts) applied in repeated coats (each coat being allowed to dry before the next is applied), will give the appearance of porcelain to the face and exposed necks and shoulders. Skin colourings can then be created with a little added fabric paint/dye prior to the final coatings. Acrylic paints can be applied to fantasy heads and grotesque images.

Clare Seeley's stumpwork miniature of Charles I when Prince of Wales is based on the 17th-century portrait by Nicholas Hilliard. Size: 6 x 5cm (2⅜ x 1⅞in)

Some panels for a box were perhaps folded or trimmed to create this composite panel, now at Fenton House. The panels would cover a box measuring about 27 x 22 x 14cm (10⅝ x 8¾ x 5½in) including the inner and outer faces of two front doors, and the fronts for some inner drawers. Courtesy of the National Trust Photographic Library/Jonathon Gibson.

ROYAL MINIATURES

A portrait of Henry VIII by Hilliard and another of Anne of Cleves by Holbein inspired this dual project. It is suggested each be worked not larger than 8cm (3in) in diameter. The soft sculpture technique used for these heads is employed throughout the book, but note that those of Henry and Anne are large in comparison with others. The illustrated needlelace techniques also have a general application, and should be referred to when working other projects. A variety of padding techniques are described elsewhere, but the raising effects for Henry and Anne rely almost entirely on layer(s) of needlelace and a little felt.

Transfering the Designs to Fabric

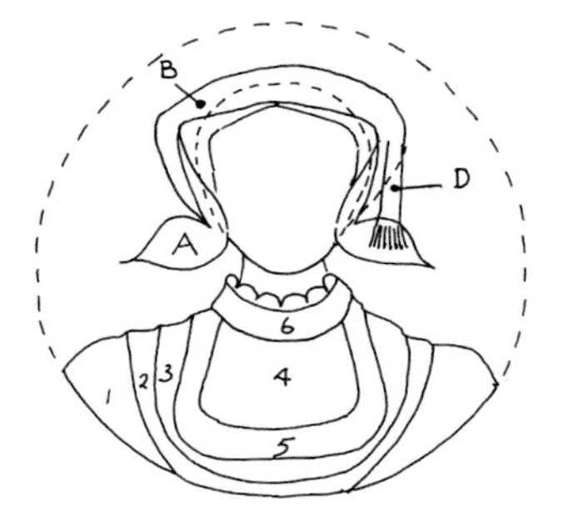

Trace or photocopy the designs, varying the size as desired, then transfer these to the unbleached and unwashed calico ground as already described, using gold fabric paint. Remember that the lines painted on the edge of the figure will lie inside those on the design drawing, and ignore hats, hands and any other features that fly above the ground fabric – these are never painted on the ground. The numbers and letters code on the Anne of Cleves design is for guidance when working and applying the needlelace.

Diluted blue silk dyes coat the ground above the shoulder line. Moisten the calico; apply the dye; allow it to dry, and then iron the fabric to set the dye, as already described. Metallic fabric paints, applied to dry calico, coat the figures below the shoulder line in colours that match the costume (the coloured dyes are mixed with white metallic pearl to achieve a sheen). The pale grey areas will be visible through Henry's lattice-work waistcoat on the finished embroidery.

HEADS AND FACES

Iron the ground fabric when all paints/dyes are dry. Next, stretch and keep the fabric permanently taut in a round embroidery frame while working the heads (and the remainder of the embroidery). To work each head separately, paint the shape/size in gold outline on a separate piece of lightweight calico and stretch this in its own small round embroidery frame; now proceed as described below.

Using well-washed lightweight calico, on the cross, cut an oval about 6mm (¼in) larger than the required head. Before cutting, run a gathering thread around the shape (knot the end of the gathering thread) about 3mm (⅛in) outside the head size. Draw up, turn under, and knot the end of the gathering thread to produce a calico shape similar in size to the head on the design drawing. The shape of the head on the embroidery is determined as you bring the needle and matching thread up through the ground just outside the gold outline, catching the slip with a tiny invisible stitch, then return through the ground in exactly the same position.

Start by stitching around the chin and up to the mouth (midway between chin and eyes). Insert soft filling into the slip, particularly the chin, and form a dot stitch at the mouth position. Continue stitching up both sides of the head to the eyes (midway between chin and top of head); pack in more filling to meet that already in place, and anchor it with two dot stitches in the eye positions. Continue stitching around the top of the head, packing in the last soft filling before completion. The stitches around the slip will be barely visible if the head is well padded. To improve the modelling of a head, insert a needle through the slip to lift up and stir the filling.

Work a chain stitch (see page 54) at each eye, starting at outer corner (a) and finishing near nose (b). Draw the thread down tightly at the finish of each stitch to form a well-defined bridge for the nose. Keep the chain stitches horizontal. To open the eye, pull down the bottom thread of the chain stitch and anchor it with a dot stitch (c). A French knot forms the pupil. A simple angled straight stitch is usually sufficient for an eyebrow, but stem stitch is used for Henry. (For smaller heads, the dimensions given in Step 1 must be reduced.)

The character will change dramatically if eyebrows are incorrectly angled, positioned or shaped. A bullion knot forms Henry's mouth, but a more delicate straight stitch is sufficient for Anne; both are anchored in a slight curve with a dot stitch. Two parallel bullion knots (with their tops opposite the eye) are anchored in a crescent shape to form ears. Within a precise shape, masses of Pekin knots (see page 54) describe Henry's beard and moustache.

NEEDLELACE FOR CLOTHING

Embroidery and needlelace combine to create stumpwork, and when they are in perfect harmony the result can be a successful composition. Whereas embroidery stitches are worked through a permanent ground fabric, the detached buttonhole stitches of needlelace are formed above the upper surface of a temporary foundation fabric. Each piece of needlelace, made to a required shape and size, has a continuous double thread around the edge (the cordonnet) which is couched to the upper surface of the temporary foundation. These couching stitches are the only ones to penetrate the surface of the temporary foundation. The rows of detached buttonhole stitches that form the piece of needlelace link with each other and with the cordonnet on every edge. The completed piece of needlelace is finally freed from its temporary foundation by cutting and teasing away the couching stitches on the underside of the foundation.

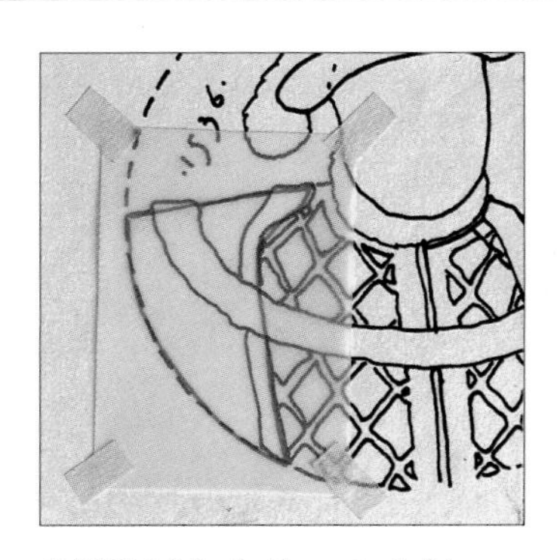

1 PVC tablecloth material is used here for the temporary foundation. A convenient size will be 15cm (6in) square. Baste this to two layers of cotton backing. Trace each needlelace shape from the design drawing. You will need fine pointed needles for couching and fine tapestry or ball point needles when making needlelace.

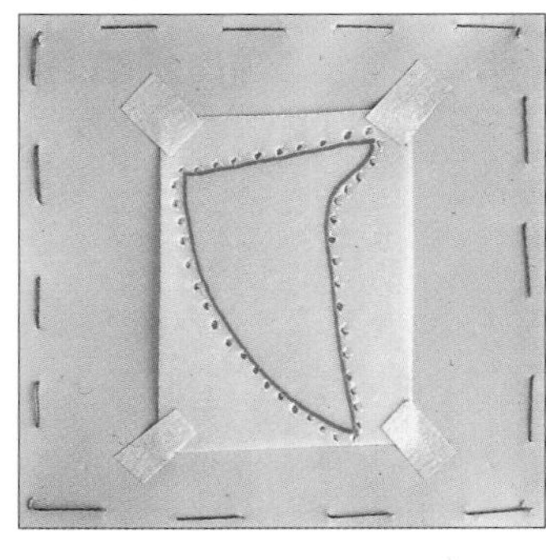

2 With the tracing over the smooth surface of the foundation fabric, and with a soft pad beneath, pierce small holes with a stiletto through the PVC, just outside the edge of the traced shape (or a little further outside if the finished needlelace has to fit over a padded area). Discard the tracing once the shape is outlined with holes.

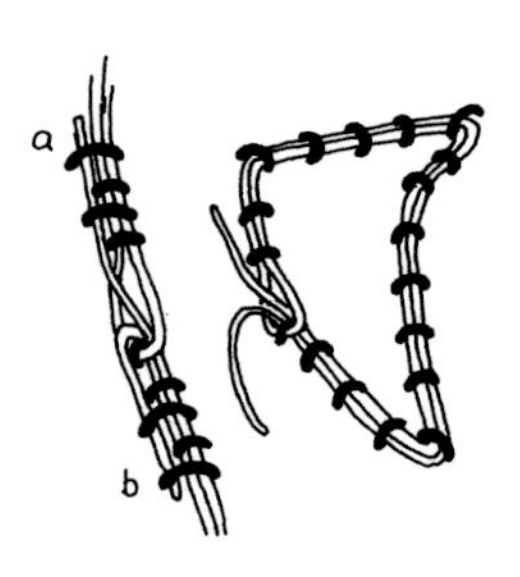

3 Couch the double cordonnet thread over the line of pierced holes. Knot the end of the couching thread and bring the needle up through the foundation, making the first couching stitch in the loop of the cordonnet. Continue couching around the shape then thread and couch the end of the cordonnet as shown.

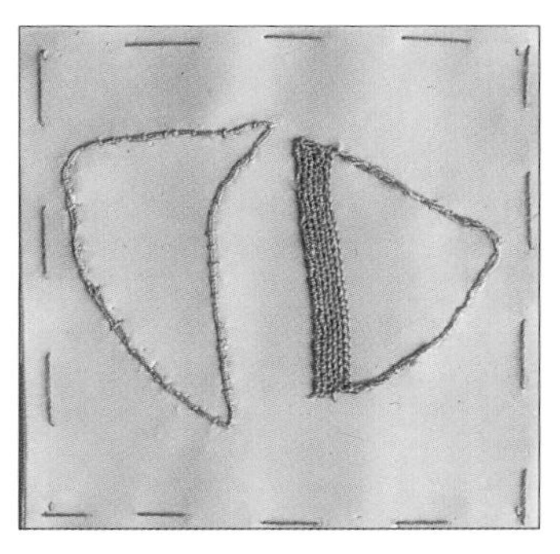

4 These are the laid cordonnets for the two parts of Henry's cloak. Both shapes are to be filled with corded buttonhole stitch (below). The diagram shows the starting point S. Follow a chosen edge when working needlelace. On completion, the edges may be buttonholed for a neat (though heavier) finish.

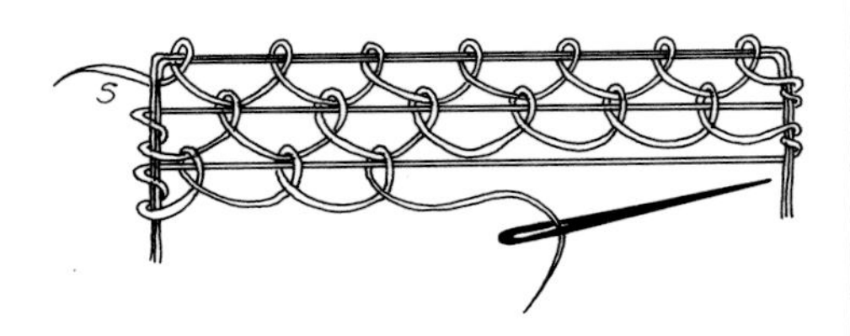

Worked experimentally, and with considerable expertise in lace, Cynthia Voysey's Elizabeth I *is remarkably inventive. Cynthia uses a 120 Honiton thread for buttonhole stitching on the edges of the diaphanous cloak of silk gauze, adding tiny beads for picots. A 150 glazed cotton was used to create the large needlelace collar, which was smocked prior to removal from its backing and gathered while being applied to the figure. The hair is formed with long pieces of thread purl, couched at frequent intervals over satin stitching. Brass wire, brass and antique beads, and gold threads were added for the final embellishments. Size: 7 x 6.3cm (2¾ x 2½in)*

Henry's Lattice-Work Waistcoat

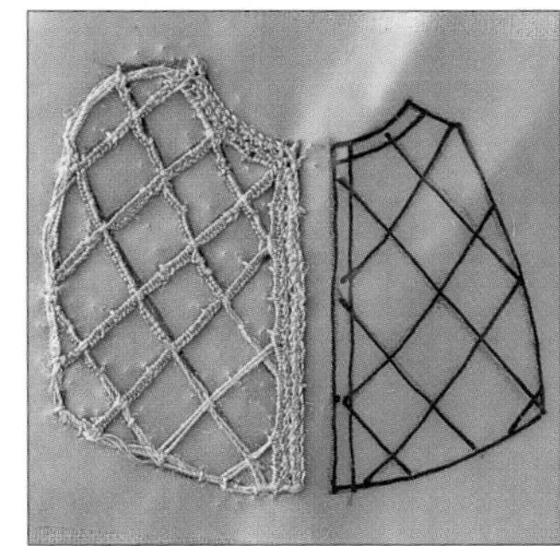

1 Matt adhesive film is used here as an alternative temporary foundation. This is a transparent self-adhesive film, attached to a backing paper which is discarded. A tracing of the two-part waistcoat is trapped between the adhesive film and a larger cotton backing. Using an extra-long double thread, couch the cordonnet over the traced lines, following diagrams A, B, and C in sequence. Corded buttonhole fills the narrow space around collar and closing edges. Buttonhole stitch over the lines of lattice threads, finishing with the outer cordonnet. Keep the buttonhole knots on the bottom edge throughout, and pass the working thread beneath the lace at points of intersection.

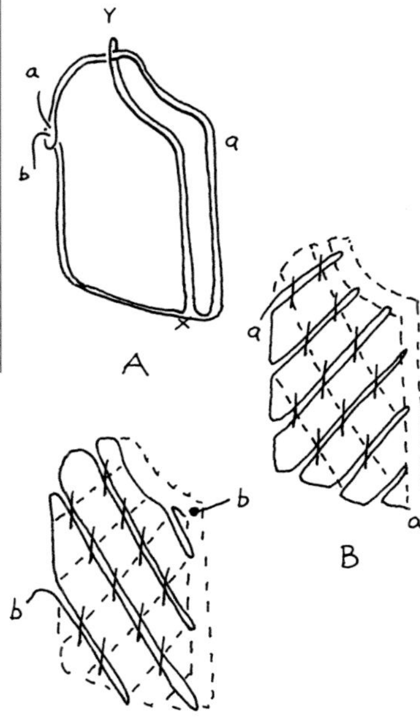

2 Frequent couching is required to retain the shape of the cordonnet, particularly at trellis intersections and changes of direction. One cordonnet thread leaves and returns to point x after wrapping over the cordonnet at y. After completing the edge cordonnet, use thread 'a' to complete the route shown on diagram B; couch the thread on the outward journey then wrap it over the cordonnet before threading it through all the couching stitches on the return journey. Repeat with thread 'b', following diagram C.

The Hat

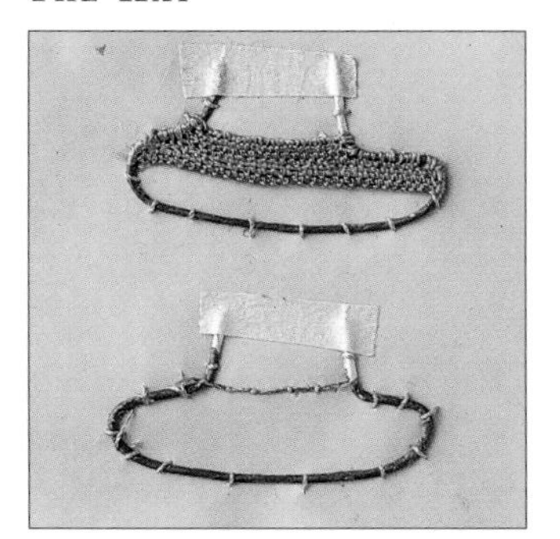

Bend rust-proof wire to a hat brim shape; paint it with matching acrylic paint or wrap with thread; couch it to the temporary foundation and wrap a double cordonnet thread around the tails to close the gap. Masking tape over the tails prevents threads catching. Fill the enclosed space with corded buttonhole. The wire tails will be inserted through the ground fabric at x-x (see page 26) and then bent and stitched behind the head. The back edge of the brim must be correctly positioned and stitched through the padded head.

DECORATIONS AND ASSEMBLING

When applying needlelace to the embroidery, use a matching thread and small, close, invisible stitches. The roll-over method of applying the needlelace described here achieves a pleasing rounded quality to an important edge of the work. When small beads are attached to the face of the needlelace, it is often necessary to back the lace with a fine fabric (such as silk organza) in a matching colour.

Several pieces are here attached to the temporary PVC foundation: the crown of Henry's hat (top right); Henry's ruff, which will need an added lengthwise central gathering thread (middle); Anne's bodice (section 4, page 26), made in a mixture of corded buttonhole and treble Brussels stitch and with a simplified loop picot edge, and the couronnes for Henry's chain, being made on the left.

Always start by applying the lowest layer of needlelace (here it is the waistcoat), and work upwards in succeeding layers. Plan a working order. To raise the cloak, attach a piece of matching felt to the ground beneath it. With the back uppermost, stitch the cloak along the visually important shoulder line, prior to rolling it over in the next stage. Small pearls (or beads) can now be applied to the waistcoat, the stitches taken through the ground.

This early 17th-century New Testament illustrates David with his harp on the front cover, Abraham preparing to sacrifice Isaac on the back cover, and a butterfly, rose, bird, and tulip in descending order on the spine. Size: 11.5 x 9cm (4½ x 3½in); courtesy of the Bodleian Library, University of Oxford (ref. Douce Bib Eng N.T. 1625. g1).

The cloak can now be rolled over to its correct position and stitched along the outer edge. Embroider two rows of pendant couching along the closing edge(s) to suggest fur. The narrow needlelace ruff is manipulated and stitched in position in the gap between chin and waistcoat collar. Take the wire ends of the hat brim through the ground and secure them; position the back edge of the brim correctly, and stitch it through the padded head. Finish by applying the chain of office. Henry's hat crown is stitched to the ground over his padded head and also to the back edge of the brim.

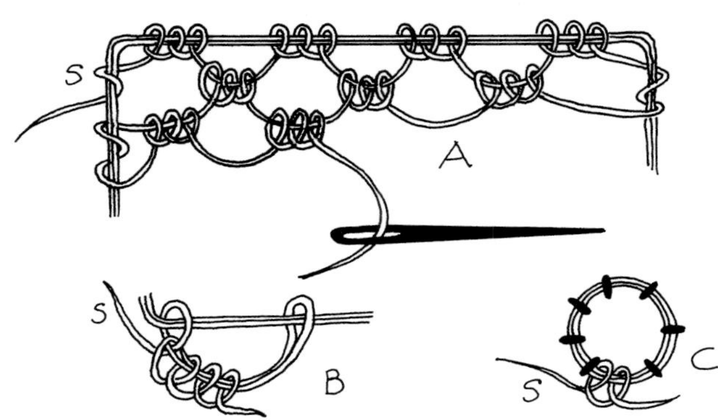

These diagrams describe treble Brussels stitch (A), a simplified loop picot (B), and a couronne (a buttonhole ring) (C).

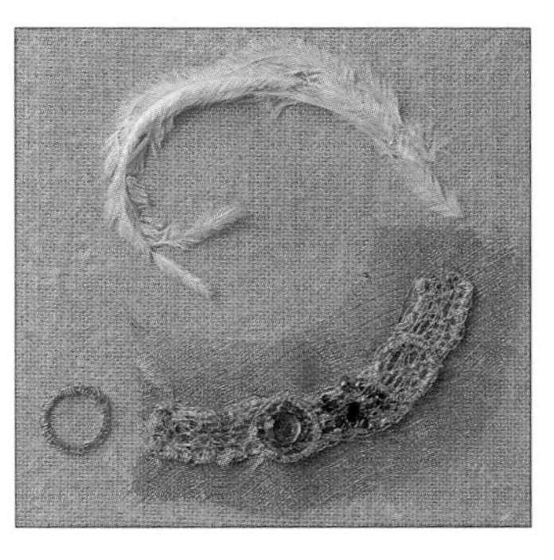

Henry's chain is corded buttonhole stitch in metallic gold machine thread. After being freed from the temporary foundation, it is backed with organza to receive beads and couronnes. Curved and overlapping fragments of ostrich feather are individually stitched to follow the upper surface of Henry's hat brim.

Completing Anne of Cleves

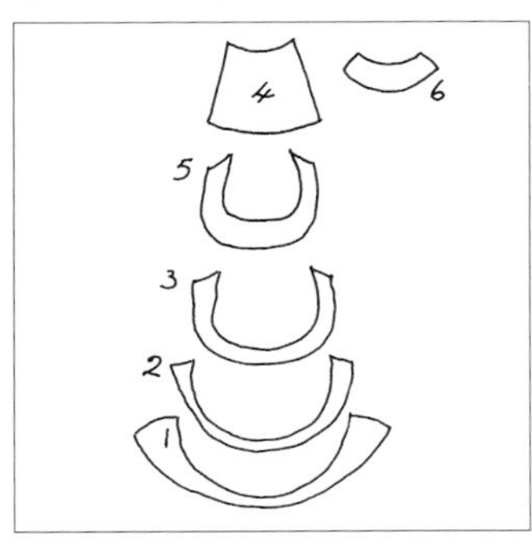

These six needlelace shapes form Anne's dress. The numbers, matching those on the design drawing, also indicate the sequence for application to the embroidery. Lightly pad (4) with white felt. Numbers 1, 2, 3, 5, and 6 are worked in corded buttonhole stitch.

Matching felt in the shape of the hair style has been applied (right); long directional satin stitches cover the felt (left); knotted threads, pulled through the ground, form a hair plait (right); needlelace (B) is being stitched to the ground to overlap the head.

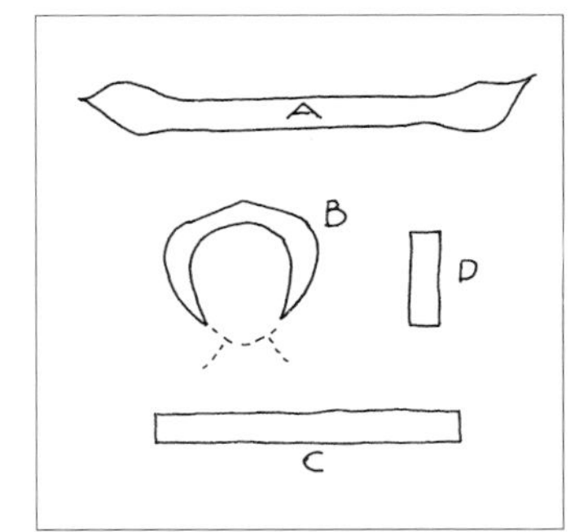

Section A of Anne's head-dress is too heavy worked in needlelace. Bobbin lace might be satisfactory. Our suggestion is white organza with a machine-stitched edge overpainted with acrylic paint. Work B, C, and D in treble Brussels stitch.

After B is fully stitched, A can be applied. It is stitched to B on its back edge and then projects like a bonnet. A single stitch anchors each point to the ground fabric. Gold needlelace sections C and D decorate the bonnet and plait.

MISCELLANEOUS FIGURATIVE TECHNIQUES

Necks and shoulders are often obscured by clothing, but even when visible they may simply be painted on the ground, as with Anne of Cleves. When exposed necks and shoulders need padding, they are constructed separately from thin card, lightweight calico (cut on the cross) and soft filling. A few hidden stitches subsequently anchor this padded form to the ground. Legs and feet are made in the same way, but the soft filling is usually omitted.

1 Making the shape slightly smaller than that on the design, cut it from thin card. Glue a traced shape to the card as a guide. Cut the piece of calico a little larger than the card shape and snip around the edges.

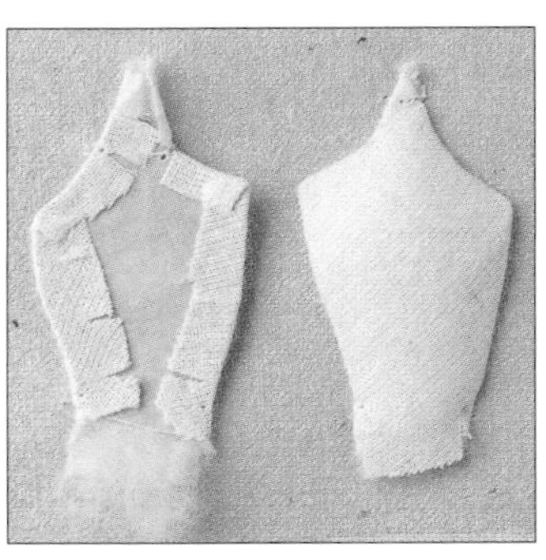

2 Stretch the calico over the card and glue the side allowances to the underside of the card with white glue. When the glue has set, insert soft filling between card and calico.

Here, the card shape ends before it reaches the chin, but the calico extends upwards behind the head. The needlelace bodice is stitched to the ground beyond the card edges, while the smaller decorative needlelace pieces are subsequently stitched to the bodice.

The card base stops short of the hair line on this semi-profile miniature, but the calico continues upwards and partly covers the padded head slip; the join is hidden by felt and satin stitching. Bullion knots and thread purl form the crown.

LADY IN A GREEN HAT

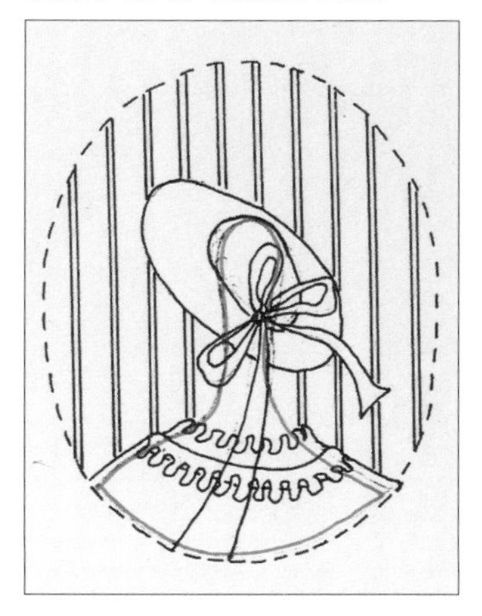

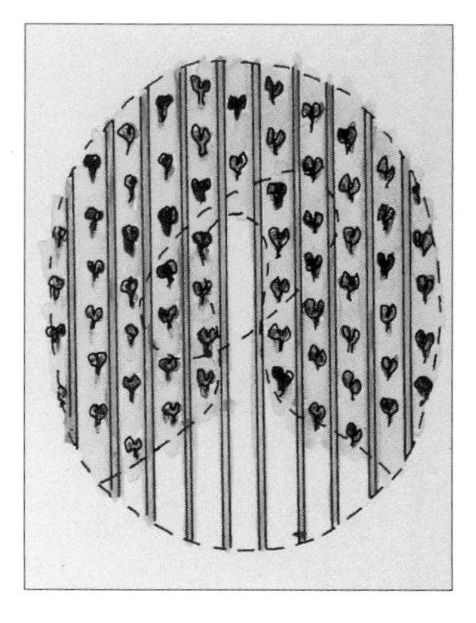

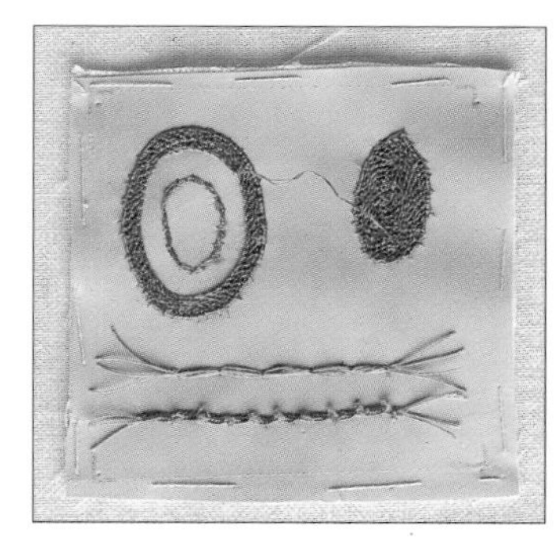

3 Add a beading wire to the hat brim cordonnet; buttonhole over this (knots inwards) then continue round and round to meet the inner cordonnet. Completely fill the hat crown with corded buttonhole. To form the decorative band, couch a beading wire with numerous threads to a temporary foundation (as for a cordonnette); buttonhole over these, but draw out short tufts of core threads at regular intervals as work proceeds.

1 Needlelace, a neck ruff and hat bow of free machine embroidery, and a transfer-dyed satin ground fabric combine to create this Victorian lady. The red lines on the design drawing show the outline of the form, made from calico-covered padded card. In common with other miniatures illustrated here, the oval has a height of 6.5cm (2½in).

2 The transfer pattern is a mirror image of the design; apply the transfer dyes to a porous paper and allow to dry. With the painted surface face down over a synthetic ground fabric, a hot iron will transfer the colours from paper to fabric. Now add painted gold design lines to the ground to define the position of head, neck, and shoulders.

4 Double rows of machine stitching follow the vertical lines and the satin ground is backed with felt. Choose a suitable needlelace stitch for the gown. Work a cordonnette on the neck line and draw out tufts of core thread at intervals as a decoration.

HEADS IN PROFILE

Those confident of good results might attempt to work profile heads directly onto the ground, but we recommend making them separately and transferring them to the main embroidery when they are nearer completion and of proven quality. Work as already described for a front-facing head, and start by preparing the oval of calico, complete with gathering thread, drawn up and turned under, and of a size that matches the profile head on the design.

1 Paint a clear and accurate outline of the profile and head on the ground and a separate fabric; as always, keep this inside the shape on the design drawing. When stitching, bring the needle up just outside the painted line and make a tiny stitch into the edge of the slip as the needle returns through the ground/separate fabric in the same position.

2 Begin stitching at the forehead and work down the face, finishing at the neck. Before making each stitch, manipulate the hem of the slip, forcing it to adopt the shape of the profile. Push soft filling into the shape, particularly the nose and chin. Stitch around the crown and back of the head, adding filling as work proceeds. Mark the positions of the eye and mouth with dot stitches. Add a chain stitch (over the dot) to form the eye, a straight stitch (with a curve) for the mouth and eyebrows.

3 The ears are made with a pair of bullion knots, the top of the ear being positioned opposite the eye. A piece of felt has been applied, carefully shaped to define the hair style; completely cover this with directional straight stitches, and continue to add curls, plaits or other special details.

If you work the head on a separate piece of fabric, cut it away and apply it to the main embroidery before starting work on the hair. When cutting, leave a 3mm (⅛in) allowance; gather this beneath the head, cutting away any excess bulk, and lace it across the back. After carefully positioning the head on the main embroidery, firmly stitch it in position with three or four hidden stitches. Now work the hair as described.

Making Hands and Arms

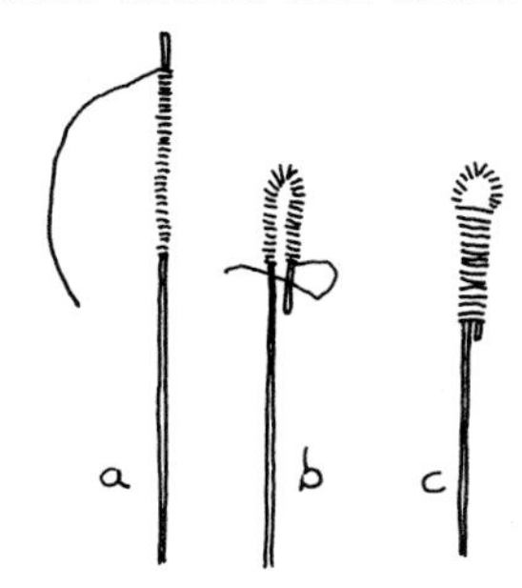

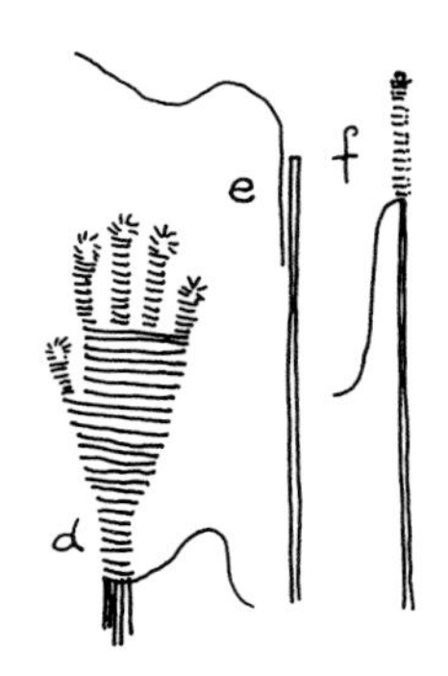

Five pieces of wire a little longer than the arm are required for each hand and arm. Use No 33 paper-covered cake icing wire, or wire of a similar thickness. Each wire is bound with silk thread for about 1cm ($\frac{3}{8}$in) at one end (a). Bend the bound end of wire, anchoring the loose thread in the bent wire (b). Overbind the bent wire as shown in (c). Leave a long thread on one finger and use this to bind the four fingers and thumb together as at (d). For a smaller hand, do not bend the fingers. Using white glue, bond the thread to the tip of the wire (e) then bind the wire slightly further than the length of a finger (f). Assemble the hand as illustrated at (d). The accompanying illustration shows the smaller hand.

When binding, start by joining the four fingers together side by side; add the thumb with further binding; continue to bind to the wrist. Twist the five arm wires together and bend them at the elbow to match the required arm length. If the arm is bare, continue to wrap the wires with silk thread to the required sculptural shape. An unwrapped wire arm within a sleeve provides fixing choices and improves the sculptural quality of the figure. The arm need only be stitched to the ground above the elbow, allowing greater freedom to raise and manipulate the wrist.

Hide the arm fixings beneath sleeves and elsewhere, and stitch firmly. When fixings are visible, match the wrapping thread. With care, the fingers can be bent to grip instruments and implements. The mandolin in this miniature is carved from wood, covered with aluminium for strength, and finished in thin leather. The strings also fix the instrument to the ground fabric.

MACHINE EMBROIDERED DECORATIONS

Small fragments of machine embroidery make ideal trimmings for needlelace clothing as well as for certain three-dimensional objects. The fragments are tiny, but they are worked on a piece of fabric large enough to be safely handled when using the sewing machine or to fit into a small round frame for machine embroidery. Normal machine stitching mode (foot in position and feed dogs operative) is preferable when making the clothing decorations for

The busy gardener of Summer Celebrations, *worked in traditional stumpwork techniques, is surrounded by larger-than-life fuchsias and a formal garden, complete with topiary in machine embroidery. The design continues onto the edges of the panel, which also incorporate commemorative information. Size: 20cm (8in) square*

Baroque Reflections (see page 69). Free running stitch is necessary for the cabbages and fuchsias, so set the dials at 'o'; lower or cover the feed dogs; remove the foot or use a darning foot; and stretch the silk organza in a round frame in machine embroidery mode. To avoid excessive build up of texture, keep the fabric moving when the machine is running. Trace the shapes on tissue paper and pin or baste this to the upper surface of the fabric as the stitching guide.

When the stitching is complete, tear and tease away all traces of the paper. The tiny shapes are carefully cut away close against the machined edge. For the past decade or more, embroiderers have singed the edges of such fragments when using appropriate materials, such as silk organza, and some use a very small electric soldering iron for the purpose. If these methods are used, hold the tiny embroidered fragments with metal pliers and work well away from all inflammable materials and in a safe non-combustible environment. The edges of fabric can be decorated, and sometimes sealed, with acrylic paint, or the fabric can be backed with iron-on vilene to prevent fraying.

Brassicas

Organza is stretched over a spun cotton ball and held in position with whipped threads; this forms the heart. The outer leaves are worked as a circular group; shown with the tissue paper pattern almost intact (left) and partly cut and singed (right). The outer leaves are finally wrapped and stitched over the heart. (The finished picture is on page 20.)

Clothing Decorations

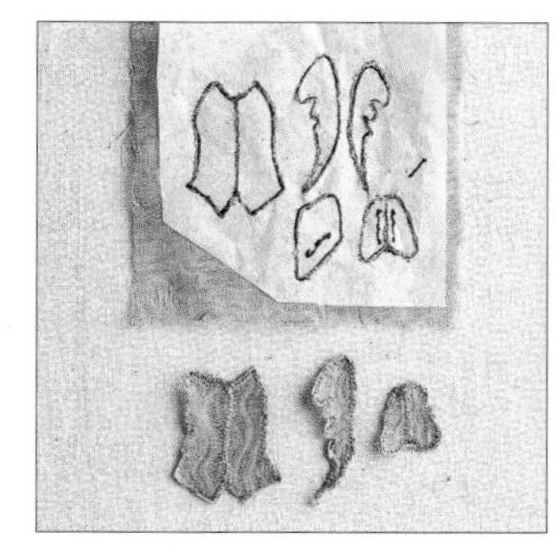

The musicians on the mirror frame (see page 69) wear machine-stitched waistcoats and needlelace jackets, decorated with machine embroidered revers, cuffs, and tails, all applied over the padded figure in that order. A metallic fabric was used, and the cut edges were sealed and decorated with acrylic paint. The machined edges are fragile and it is essential to take care when they are stitched over the padded needlelace figure.

Fuchsias & Leaves

A group of four petals stitched over an oval bead form a core. Threads for stamens pass through the hole in the bead. An outer group of long pointed petals, stitched over the core, give the distinctive fuchsia shape. Large and small groups of leaves, loosely applied and in overlapping layers, create plant-like forms. Silk organza is the ideal fabric.

CHAPTER THREE

RAISED FIGURES ON FABRIC

Stumpwork is akin to sculpture, but instead of chiselling away stone or wood, or modelling with clay, scraps of soft padding or loose filling materials are built up on the ground fabric in varying thicknesses before being covered with decorative needlelace or embroidered slips to create figurative images in relief. The thickness of the needlelace or embroidered slip alone will sometimes provide sufficient relief, but the embossing can gradually be increased with added layers of felt, or made bolder still by trapping polyester filling between the felt and the ground fabric. The wire arm achieves further foreground relief, while accurate shapes formed with card, calico and polyester filling (page 32) provide the alternative raising method for exposed necks, shoulders and legs.

Because stumpwork is built up in layers, it is good practice to plan a working order when starting the embroidery, although this becomes second nature as experience develops. The padded figurative shape is created inside the painted design outline, which is transferred from the design drawing as described on page 14. Embroiderers wanting to produce a figurative design can trace a bold outline from almost any figurative illustration, while a particular stance can be photographed with the help of a friend who is willing to pose. Costume can be researched in books and museums, and subsequently added to the figurative outline. Always remember to make the painted outline on the fabric slightly smaller than the image on the design drawing; this ensures that the finished image matches the design drawing in size while also masking the painted outlines. Aim for a maximum figure size of 10cm (4in), or a smaller size of 7cm (2¾in), or less, if the design includes several figures. The construction of a number of artefacts related to figurative work are described in this section.

Clare Seeley's Le chapeau rose*, modelled on a painting by Henri Lebasque, is worked mainly in needlelace, but it also has a striking white collar in 'little fan' (torchon) bobbin lace. Size: 7cm (2¾in) square*

A favourite holiday beach with four children at play was the carefully chosen theme for this raised embroidery, Instow*, which marks a 50th anniversary. It incorporates needlelace, padded satin stitch, soft sculpture, wire wrapping, machine embroidery, dying, and fabric singeing – a mixture of 17th-century traditional techniques with those of the 20th century. Size: 25cm (9¾in) square*

CHOOSING A FIGURE

Some figurative illustrations or postures will not translate into satisfactory relief images; some do so with comparative ease, while others are complex but workable. The limbs of an obviously workable figure will all be visible, and none will be unduly distorted by posture or angle of view. Overlapping or intertwining limbs give rise to a more complex project, and one which can prove unworkable in extreme cases. Before starting work on a figure, study it in detail and plan a working order; a little thought at this stage will save much time later. A few examples follow.

In Autumn Gold*, the sweeping figure is in full profile except for the head; this is almost front facing and the left ear is visible. The right arm is hidden from view behind the body. The brush, formed from numerous silk-wrapped wires bound together, sweeps machine-stitched organza leaves, edged in metallic gold threads. Size: 16.5 x 12cm (6½ x 4½in)*

STANDING FIGURE

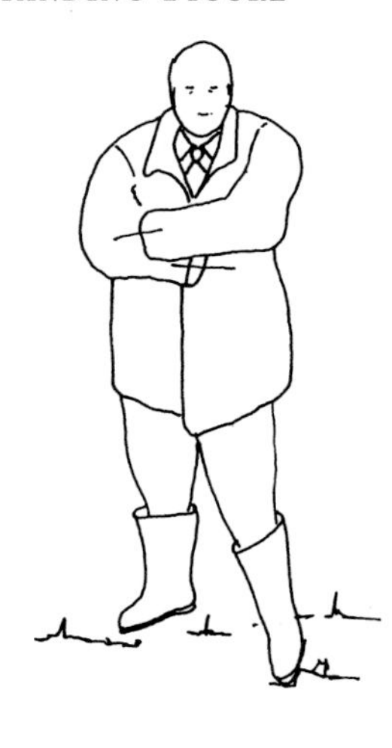

This front-facing figure will pose few problems, but the degree of success will only be known when the silk-bound wire arms, felt padding, needlelace sleeves, and stick are all stitched in position, almost at the point of completion.

WORKING FIGURE

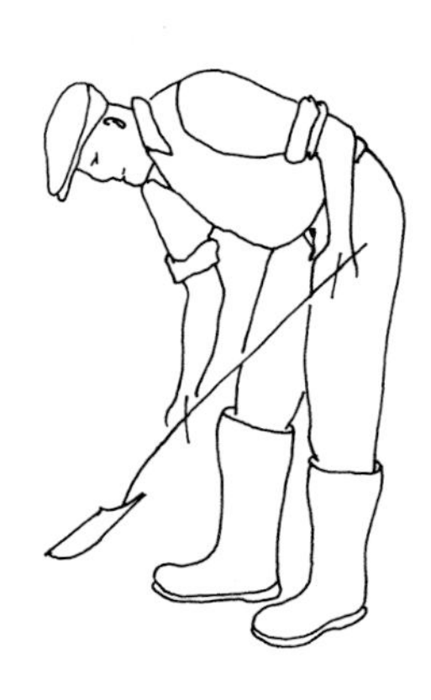

The slight twist on the body, the angle of the head, and the exact stance must all be captured to achieve success. It is more difficult than the standing figure, but achievable when using silk-bound wire arms.

SEATED FIGURE

This seated figure with folded legs is an advanced project. The upper and lower halves of each leg must be completely straight (bones do not bend). A chair, or rock, may be necessary to make the figure 'sit' in the composition.

CROUCHING FIGURE

Because one part of each leg is not visible, this crouching figure may not translate satisfactorily into stumpwork. It can be attempted as a time-consuming exercise, but with no guarantee of a successful outcome.

A WORKING ORDER

The golfer in *The Edge of The Rough* is 9cm (3½in) tall. Adjust the drawing to the correct size (your local photocopying agency can do this for you) before transferring the design to fabric. All dyeing and machine stitching should be completed before starting to form a figure.

GOLFER

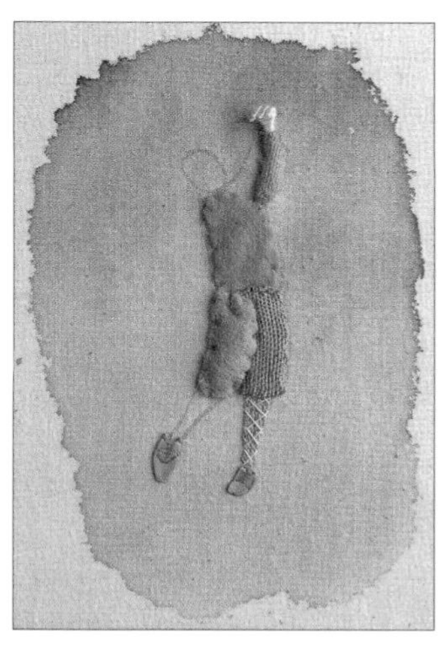

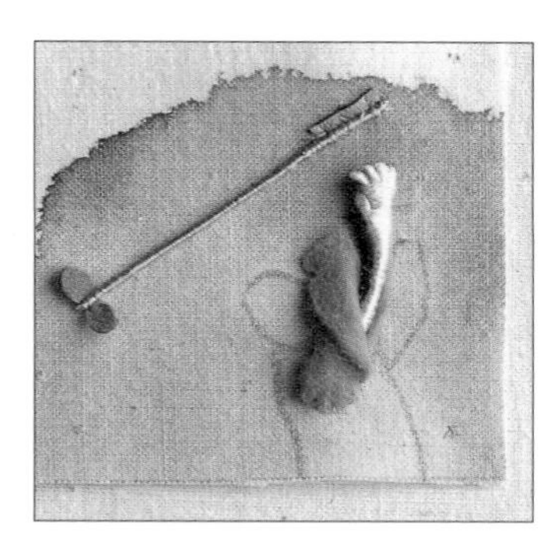

1 The left arm and leg, formed from felt, soft filling and a needlelace surface, are completed at this early stage, along with the leather shoes and embroidered stockings. The latter are embroidered on the ground in vertical rows of chain stitches (see page 54), overworked with long diagonal straight stitches. These collectively form the first stage. Work has also commenced on the next, overlapping stage; felt and soft filling have been stitched in position to form the right leg and the upper body and the two pieces of needlelace which cover these must be applied next.

2 For clarity the arm is divorced from the padded body in this illustration. Make sure the right arm is correct in length and shape before stitching it firmly in place over the needlelace body. Insert extra felt padding beneath the lower part of the arm, as illustrated. Complete by stitching the felt shape over the wire arm and then carefully stitch the final piece of needlelace in position. The golf club is formed from silk-wrapped wire, with bonded leather for the hand grip and striking end.

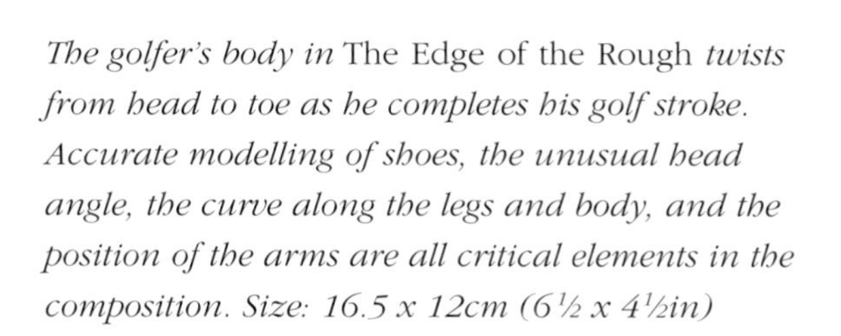

The golfer's body in The Edge of the Rough *twists from head to toe as he completes his golf stroke. Accurate modelling of shoes, the unusual head angle, the curve along the legs and body, and the position of the arms are all critical elements in the composition. Size: 16.5 x 12cm (6½ x 4½in)*

LA BOUTIQUE DE MODISTE

On this panel, an elegant 1920s lady poses in a boutique decorated in the art nouveau style. She is 12cm (4¾in) tall and, being larger than our recommended maximum, needs to be worked with sensitivity to avoid ugly results. With this in mind, fine rayon machine threads are recommended for the needlelace; tiny delicate hands are required; flimsy machined decorations are best worked on silk organza or similar fabric or hand worked with the finest of threads; minute Victorian beads are desirable (manufacturers no longer produce beads in such small sizes); excessive padding must be avoided, and very special care will be needed when attaching the needlelace gown.

Design and Ground

A panel size of about 20cm (8in) wide and 18cm (7in) deep is recommended, and a ground fabric with a rich sheen is desirable. The worked example has a composite ground; a strong bottom calico layer which also receives the design and coloured dyes, and an overlay of champagne-coloured silk organza.

The Padded Figure

The neck piece and legs are formed in card and calico (see page 32) plus a little soft filling for the neck; the shoes are painted on the calico with acrylic paint, and the stocking colour is achieved with fabric paints. The face and neck are given repeated coats of diluted white glue. Only two layers of felt are needed beneath the needlelace skirt and bodice. Note that both arms are already stitched to the ground and the needlelace sleeve has been stitched over the left arm. The head, slightly turning, and the hair, can now be worked to complete the first stage.

Needlelace Shapes

These are the seven shapes required for the needlelace dress; the edges of 4, 5, 6, and 7 slightly overlap each other when applied over the felt padding. The needlelace edges marked 'x' are stitched to the ground before being rolled over to give a high quality finish (see page 30). To avoid bulk, do not overlap the needlelace bodice and skirt at the waist. The four pink decorations on the dress are small fragments of machine embroidery on silk organza. The head band is a buttonhole bar worked over two or three threads. The belt masks the meeting of needlelace bodice and skirt.

Needlelace for the large pink hat (left) and the pale blue one (centre) is worked on a temporary foundation (see page 28). The pieces are assembled into a 3D hat on a separate vilene base, with a half bead for padding, and then attached to the main embroidery. The other hats are in relief only; they are made and applied in separate pieces with padding as necessary to achieve shape. Silk-wrapped wires form the hat stands. Mica is used in both mirrors (see page 65); the large mirror frame and dressing table are made from calico, iron-on vilene and silk dupion. These are machined together; cut away to the outer stitched edges; sealed on the edges with acrylic paint, and finally machined to the ground, trapping the mica for the mirror in the process. Size: 20 x 18cm (8 x 7in)

Minute Decorations

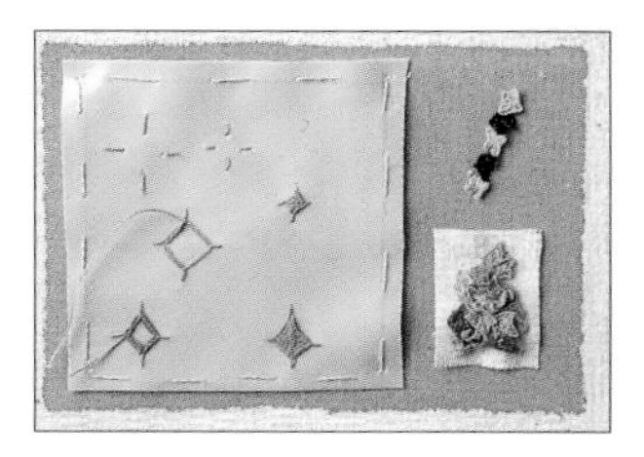

Start by working four couching stitches through a (temporary) foundation fabric as illustrated. Pass two or three threads beneath the couching stitches, then buttonhole over the threads, keeping the knot of each buttonhole stitch on the inside of the shape. Continue buttonhole stitching around the shape within the space until it is filled. Cut the couching stitches to remove the scrap of lace from the temporary foundation. These decorations can be used for flowers, textured mounds, roof tiles and possibly hair styles.

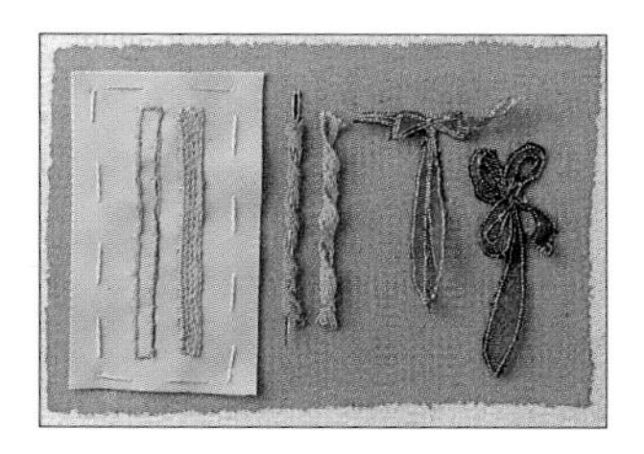

Using machine embroidery as already described, a variety of tiny decorations can be worked on organza or other decorative fabrics as illustrated on the right. This method is preferable to using purchased ribbons, which introduce a foreign quality. Hand workers might prefer to work a long narrow piece of needlelace with a beading wire in one of its long edges; having removed this strip of needlelace from its temporary foundation, twist it around a needle. See also page 33 for cordonnettes with hanging and tufted threads.

These miniatures of 18th-century ladies incorporate needlelace, silk organza, machine embroidery, and cordonnettes with tufts and hanging threads.

MUSICAL FIGURES

The seven male musicians in *Baroque Reflections* have similar characteristics, from their powdered wigs to the needlelace clothing, which is richly decorated with machine-embroidered decorations. The cellist is the only full figure. The remaining male figures are partly screened by applied music stands or drums, and these essential design features serve the practical purpose of masking the lower figure and hiding the ends of the needlelace coats. The step-by-step working instructions for the cellist should provide ample guidance when creating the remaining figures, even though the postures differ and, in the case of the conductor, there is a back view. Although the cellist is seated, there is no chair. Each figure on the mirror frame can be worked separately as a miniature stumpwork embroidery and the cellist is illustrated here in both guises on ground fabrics of slightly differing design. Refer to page 35 for methods of constructing hands and to pages 27 and 34 if reminders are needed for head construction.

HEADS WITH POWDERED WIGS

1 Stitch the head slip to the ground or make it separately. Remember to make a dot stitch at the mouth and eye positions; note that these will be off-centre on a semi-profile. Carefully control the size and facial shape by following the design outline when stitching.

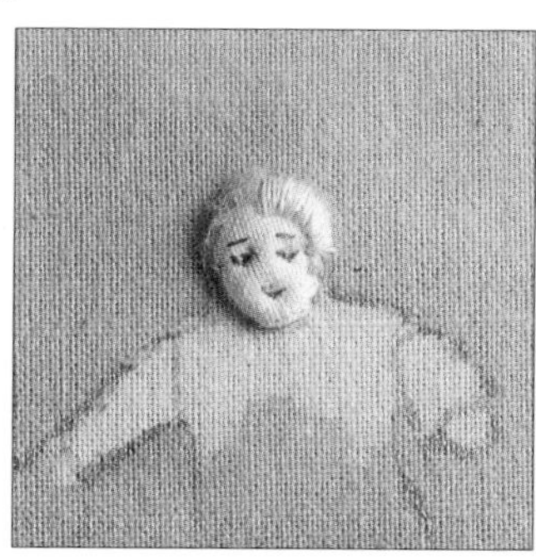

2 Use beige-coloured felt and silk or cotton threads. Embroider radiating satin stitches to cover completely the felt that describes the shape of the head. Threads for features can be in a slightly darker colour. The chain stitches for the eyes are anchored in the downward-looking position on the illustration.

3 Using the beige thread, make short lengths of thread purl (page 15). Stitch two or three of these on each side of the front-facing head, and on only one side of a head in full or half profile. The chain stitches for the eyes are now anchored in the open position.

THE CELLIST - A WORKING PLAN

The final, completed embroidery below shows the cellist on *Baroque Reflections* and the machine-embroidered costume decorations are illustrated and described on page 37.

THE CELLIST

1 The design drawing for the figures and mirror frame is on page 70. The seven needlelace shapes required for the cellist are identified here, but when pricking out the needlelace (preparing the temporary foundation and cordonnets), they should be traced from the design drawing.

2 Make and apply the card and calico legs, leather shoes, and tiny gold leather buckles. Paint the raw leather edges and the surface of the calico legs. Apply the back of the needlelace coat. Form the padded legs (upper half) with felt and soft filling. Be generous when padding the knee and gradually reduce padding to zero where the legs meet the body. Stitch the two separate pieces of needlelace over the legs to form the knee breeches. Buttonhole stitch the bottom edge of each piece of needlelace before removing it from the temporary foundation fabric.

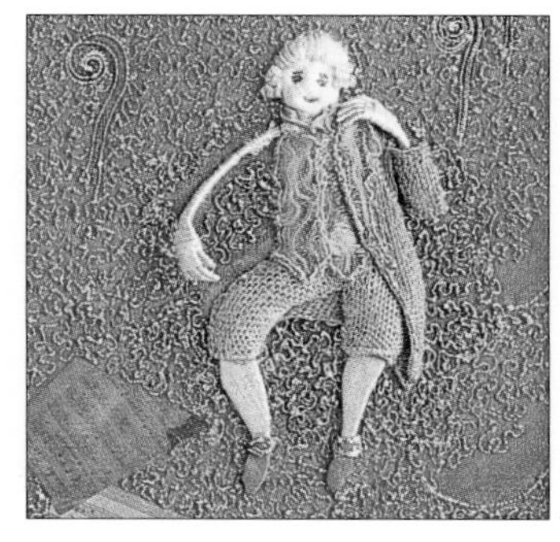

3 Apply a piece of felt similar in shape to the waistcoat as padding for the body (no soft filling required) and stitch the machine-embroidered waistcoat over the felt – all within the design lines. With great care, using tiny invisible stitches, stitch the machine-embroidered revers to the two needlelace coat fronts while the fragments are hand held. Using the roll-over method (page 30), stitch the coat fronts to the ground fabric along their outer edges; having rolled them over into their correct position, carefully stitch the shoulders to the ground. Firmly stitch the arms to the ground, cover with felt, apply the needlelace sleeves, and apply the decorative cuffs with invisible stitches. The left arm, which is only elbow length, needs lifting from the ground with felt padding(s).

4 Apply a tiny needlelace neck ruff. If the arms have been carefully controlled in shape, length and position, the cello should fit neatly in position. Fix it at the top and bottom, and elsewhere, with stitches in hidden positions (the strings can be used, with a few extra stitches). Add the bow, using similar methods. If the cello and bow are made sufficiently early, they can be used to position the arms and hands accurately on the ground, prior to stitching. Finally, apply the machine-edged music stand, keeping the stitches near to the bottom edges; add the short length of brass rod or wire, bent to an appropriate shape, and fold the fingers over to hold the bow and instrument in a realistic manner.

MUSICAL INSTRUMENTS

Make these from thin aluminium or zinc sheet, which can be cut with shears and trimmed with flat or round fine files. Smart blows on the back/centre with a rounded object form the convex shape on the face. Small holes bored in the metal receive strings and provide points for fixing the instrument to the ground fabric. Epoxy resin or other metal adhesive will bond leather to metal; follow the maker's advice and guidance. Paint the finished object with enamel or acrylic paint. Finished examples of instruments can be seen on *Baroque Reflections*.

Drums & Cymbals

The hand grip holes on the cymbals make convenient fixing points. Bond gold leather to the convex surface; trim the edges when the glue is hard; paint the leather and metal edges. Use similar techniques when making the drums and other instruments. Fixing holes can be hidden beneath the surface of the leather; two or three fixings will usually be sufficient.

Violins & Cellos

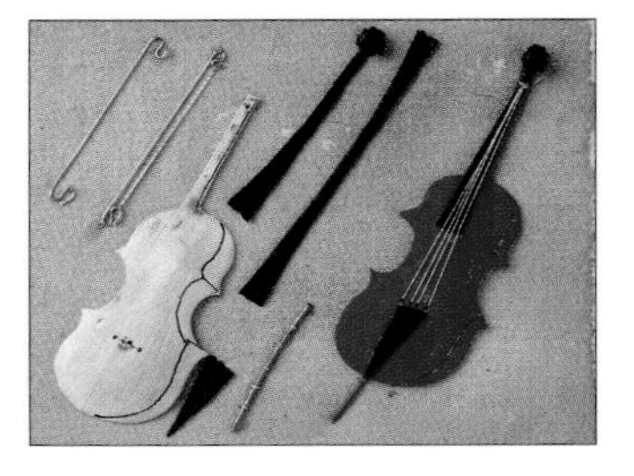

The cut edge is intricate – rely on round and flat files to achieve a good edge finish. The holes bored to receive strings will also make good fixing points. Two gold or black leather shapes are bonded to the upper convex surface; one of these is rolled over a piece of wire to create a rolled bead-like end which is the volute. Bond a wire floor spike to the back of the cello. A continuous silk thread passing through the body holes, and through a thread loop near the volute, forms the four strings. These instruments are usually slightly distorted due to the perspective shape.

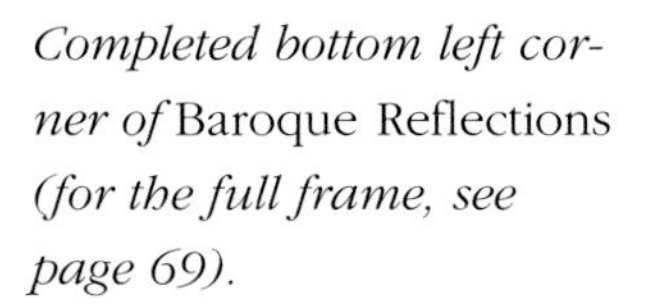

Completed bottom left corner of Baroque Reflections *(for the full frame, see page 69).*

Choirboys

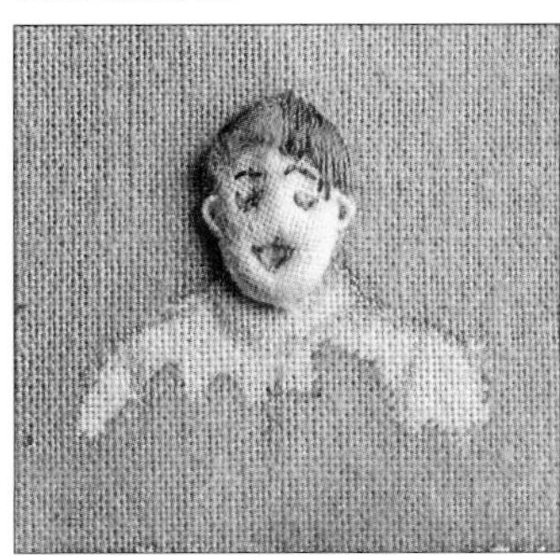

1 Form each head as already described. The choir boy will appear to sing when the chain-stitched mouth is in the open position, the eyelid is dipped, and the eyebrow is arched, so anchor the chain and straight stitches in these positions. Irregular satin stitches over a felt shape provide the urchin hair style.

2 Use a thin calico backed with lightweight vilene for the books; machine stitch the edges and the spine, and decorate the edges with acrylic paint. Stitch the calico book to the ground in a crumpled manner; apply two or three coats of acrylic paint to the calico surface to retain the crumpled shape permanently. Work on the books in turn, allowing each to overlap the previous books when fixing them in position.

EASTERN FIGURES AND HEAD-DRESSES

The soft-sculptured calico heads are treated with repeated coats of diluted white glue, with added colour in the final coats. Reasonably dark thread colours can be used for features. The angle of the eyes and eyebrows, and the shape of the open eye, are important and distinctive features.

Janet Taff's skilfully-worked Japanese lady has a gown and stole with double layers of needlelace. The stole is overworked with embroidery, and the cummerbund, black stole, fan and parasol are each intricate and innovative in their construction and application. The lady stands in a Japanese garden on a sea of minute French knots. Size: 18 x 13cm (7 x 5in)

Eastern Figures and Head-dresses

Needlelace worked in metallic gold threads, gold purl, a gold tassel and several tiny gold beads create this Thai head-dress. Make and apply the needlelace cap over the head, and insert additional soft filling. Add all the remaining details to this foundation.

Paper-covered icing wire, paper, silver leather, metallic silver threads, silver acrylic paint and tiny pearl beads make up this miniature. The head-dress is in ten separate pieces, each one being applied individually to the head or ground.

Having completely covered the head/felt shape with satin stitching, the six hair slides are added one at a time. A little additional satin stitching anchors each one in position. Care is needed in order to retain the Japanese hair style.

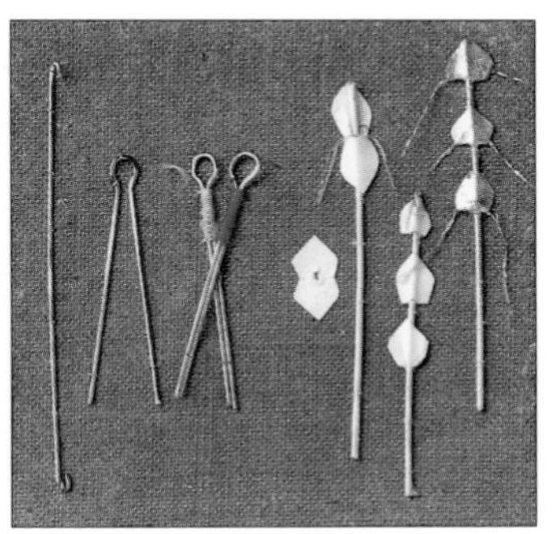

Brass wire wrapped with threads forms the hair slides for the Japanese lady. The silver head-dress has a leather tiara. The vertical features are formed with cut and folded paper fragments, which are bonded over the paper-covered wire and trap short lengths of metallic silver thread.

CHAPTER FOUR

PIN CUSHIONS, PURSES AND DECORATIVE ORNAMENTS

Decorative purses and pin cushions were much favoured by Elizabethan embroiderers, but although this liking spilled over into the 17th century, surviving stumpwork versions are rare. One example of a pin cushion, stitched on cream satin and bearing the initials and date 'A P 1647' on the back, was obviously much used and loved by its owner. Numerous similar embroideries are likely to have been created during the stumpwork craze in the middle of the 17th century. Similar articles made today will be no less vulnerable to damage and wear, but they are highly decorative and desirable for use on special occasions or to present to a discerning person to mark a unique anniversary.

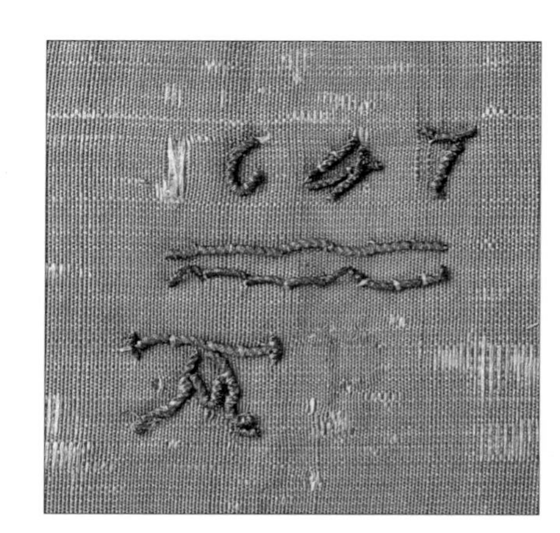

The three projects described here are all worked on the same silk dupion fabric, which has a natural colour and a slub that forms slight irregularities on the surface; the fabric should be aligned diagonally on the pin cushion and lengthwise on both purses, to avoid disturbing the designs. After transferring the designs and dyeing the fabrics, the dupion is machine stitched to a lightweight vilene backing with a metallic gold machine thread. The vilene is finally cut back to the outer machine-stitched edge.

Ensure that the silk dupion, or other chosen fabric, is free from creases and blemishes and that the design drawings have been enlarged to the desired size. The fabric must not be stretched or distorted when taped over the design drawing on the light box. After painting, the gold line is fixed with a hot iron or other approved method. Silk dyes in blue and green are allowed to coalesce on the purse fabrics; work with the fabric in a round embroidery frame to elevate it above the work surface and use a large watercolour brush. The four front leaves on the pin cushion fabric are painted on the dry fabric in a mixture of white metallic pearl and blue or green fabric paints. This colour creates a decorative shadow beneath the 'flying' wire-edged needlelace leaves, and it can be overlaid with a surface embroidery stitch if desired. Before starting to stitch, fix the dyes.

In common with similar 17th-century objects, needlelace enriches all three projects seen here. This was worked by Janet Taff, who also selected the stitches to complement our design. Hand embroidery is worked over the needlelace in the middle of the pin cushion, while needlelace and couronnes overlay the machine-embroidered feathers on the large purse.
Art nouveau pin cushion; size: 10cm (4in) square
Large peacock purse; size: 11cm (4⅜in) square
Small coin purse; size: 6 x 7cm (2¼ x 2¾in)

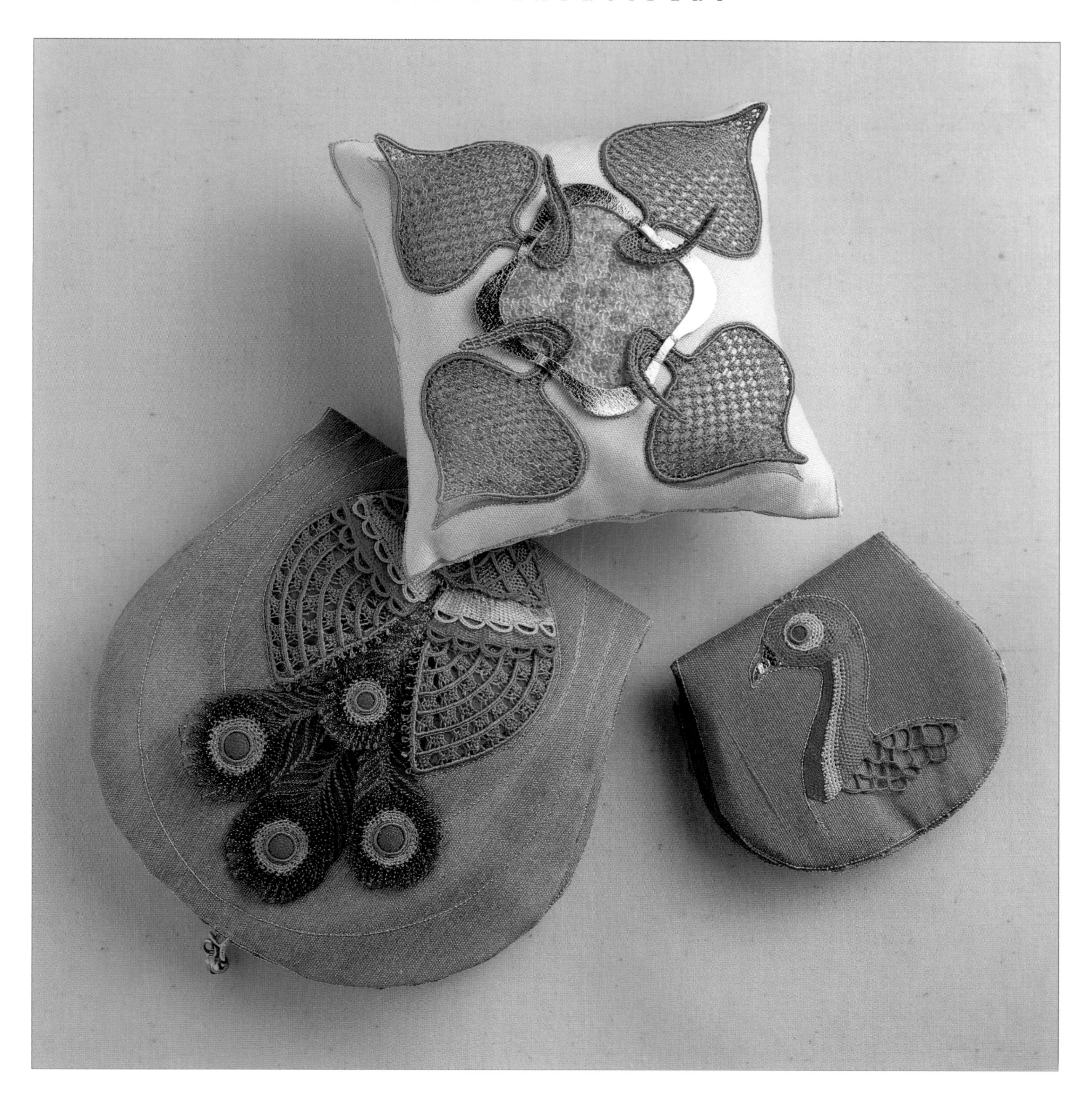

PRELIMINARY PREPARATIONS

After fixing the dyes, pin or baste the lightweight vilene to the underside of each ground fabric before starting to machine stitch. Take particular care to avoid any distortion of the ground fabric; this will alter the shapes and create continual problems, particularly during final assembly. The pin cushion is worked in one piece, but each purse has three separate ground fabrics: the outer face, an inner lining and a double-sided inner pouch.

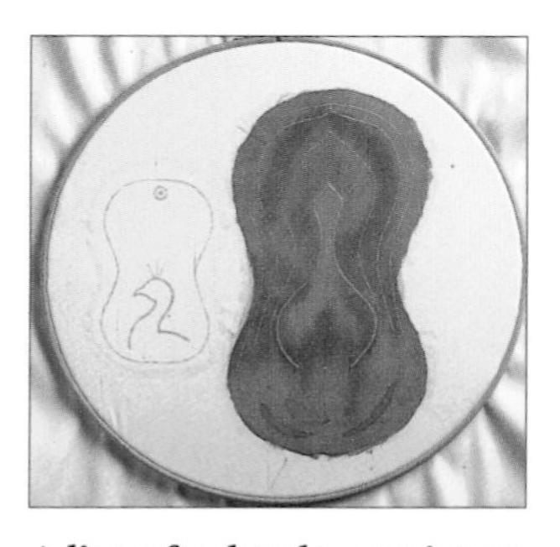

A line of colourless resist on the ground fabric beyond the edges of the purse will restrict the outward flow of the dyes. The dyes can be applied either neat or diluted and to either dry or moist fabric. When mixed with white metallic pearl, the dyes must be applied to dry fabric.

Overstitch the painted gold lines with a short straight machine stitch, maintaining accurate design shapes. Continuously lift and lower the presser foot, pivoting the fabric on the machine needle, when negotiating curves. Use a metallic gold top thread and a matching rayon bobbin thread.

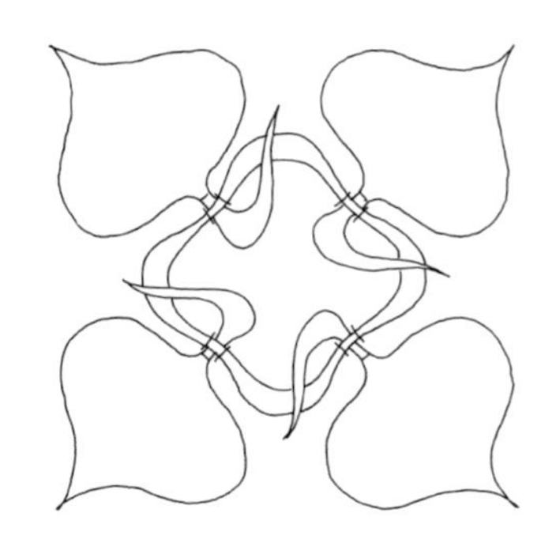

Art Nouveau Pin Cushion
Except for a little extra central detail, the designs on the front and back are identical. Add any personal initials and dates to the design drawing at the outset and transfer these to the fabric along with the design.

Silver-gilt bobbin lace (passementerie) outlines the edges of this 17th-century pin cushion, which was worked by 'AP' in 1647. Silver spangles pepper the design; flowers and seed pods, worked in needlelace, fly above the surface, while dogs and rabbits play in the margins. Size: 17 x 12cm (6¾ x 4¾in)

LARGE PEACOCK PURSE

These three design drawings for the purse show the following: A, the outer face which carries the stumpwork embroidery; B, the decorative lining of matching shape, and C, the one-piece pouch, which folds in half. The three embroideries are ladder-stitched together in the final stages, so it is important to check that the outlines precisely match each other in size when enlarged. The padded bird-like shape is formed inside the gold lines, and these should still be visible on the finished purse after the needlelace has been attached. All the needlelace pieces need to be a little larger than the same shape on the design drawing; this requires judgement after the padded shape has been formed.

Large Peacock Purse

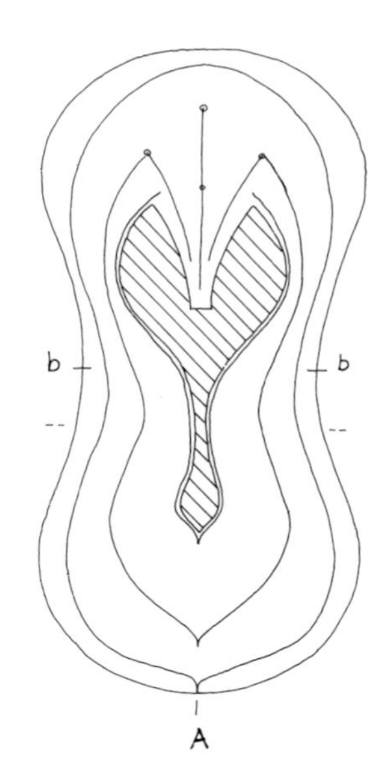

The hatched area on this outer face defines the padded 'bird' shape, formed with layers of felt. Ensure that there is only one layer on the fold of the purse 'b-b'.

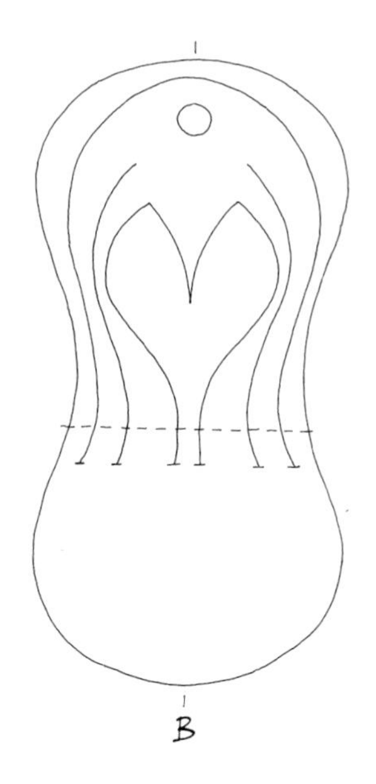

The machine-stitched gold lines on the lining mirror those on the outer face. The plain area below the horizontal line is inside the pouch.

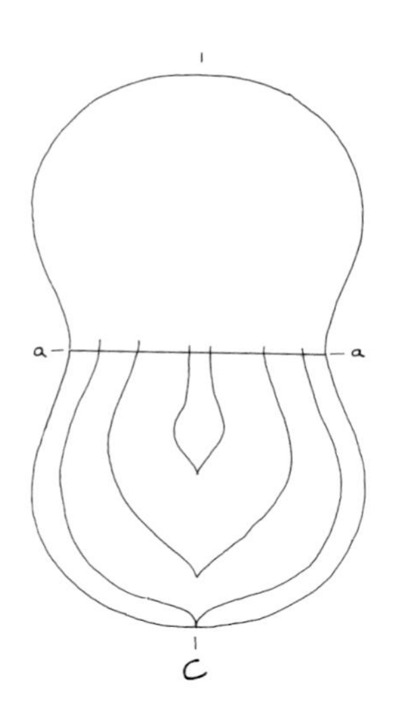

The gold lines on the decorative side of the pouch must align with those on the lining when the purse is assembled. When folded on 'a-a', the plain area lies within the pouch.

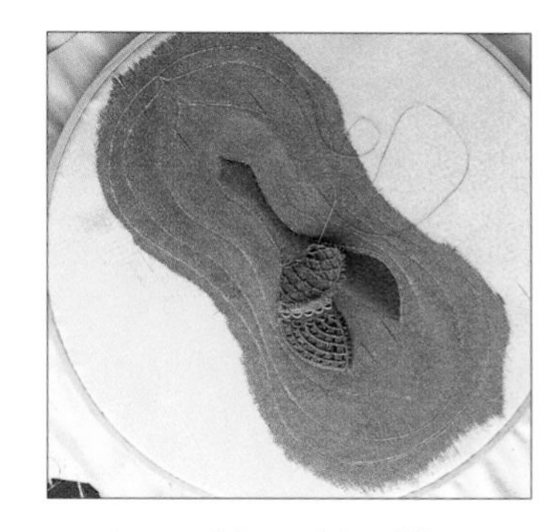

Dyeing, gold machined lines and felt padding, are all completed on the outer face, and some needlelace pieces have been attached over the padding.

PEACOCK TAIL FEATHERS

These are worked in free machine embroidery on a dark green silk organza and each one has a needlelace eye worked in single Brussels stitch, as shown. Make a tissue paper pattern as previously described, and work as instructed on pages 36–37. Hand stitch the needlelace decorations to the feather before removing the organza from the round embroidery frame. When applying the feathers to the purse, stitch the large middle one first, follow with the two side feathers, then overlay the small central one.

SINGLE BRUSSELS STITCH

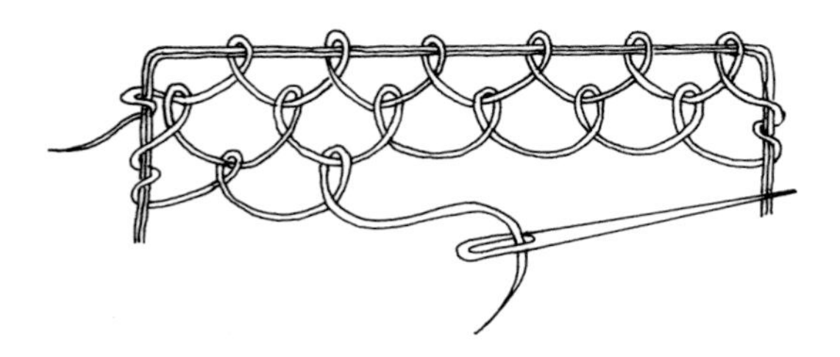

The tail feathers on Anne Smith's cockerel have the core threads from the cordonette trailing. A working design for a similar bird can be found on page 59.
Size: 7.5 x 5cm (3 x 2in)

TAIL FEATHERS

Enlarge these designs to match the purse size. Follow the lines continuously when machine stitching in free running stitch.

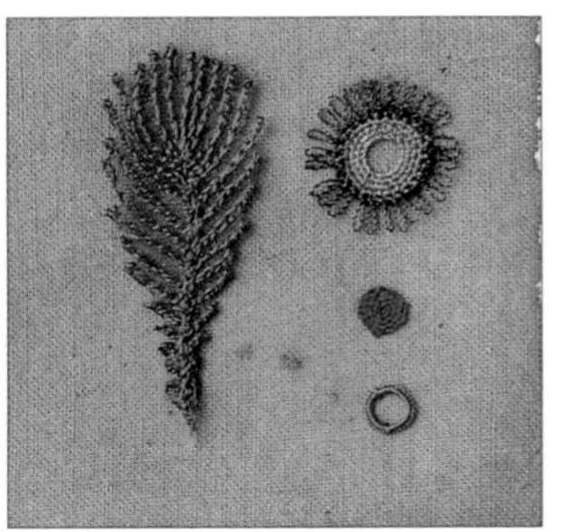

The large roundel of needlelace measures 12mm (½in), to which long pin picots are added. The small roundel measures 6mm (¼in), and the couronne is just large enough to cover its outside edge.

Cut away the surplus organza around each completed feather and singe the edge only.

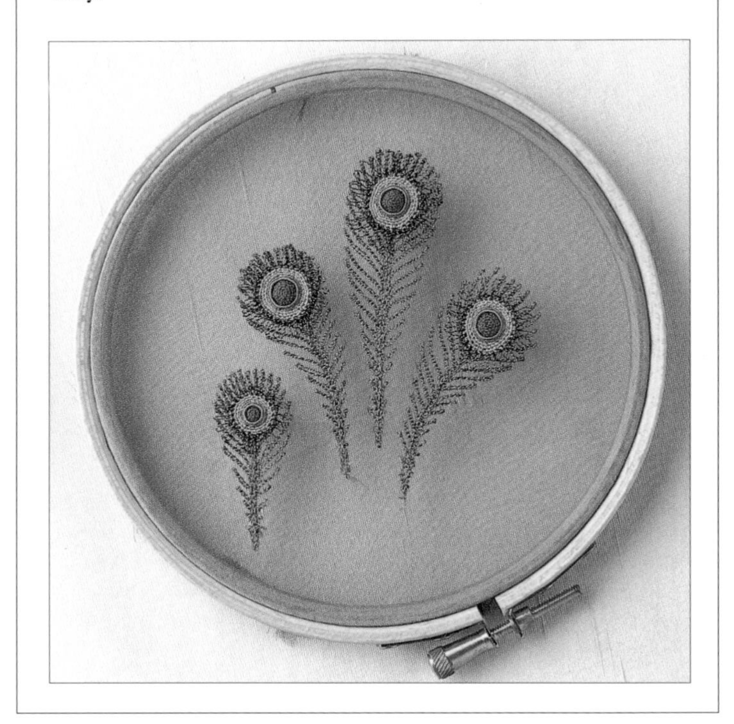

NEEDLELACE FOR THE PIN CUSHIONS AND PURSES

Rayon machine threads were chosen for the needlelace on these projects to achieve an attractive lustre, but some workers may choose a fine silk or even a cotton thread. Thin beading wire (similar to 5 amp fuse wire) is used on selected edges and elsewhere. This can either be laid with the cordonnet when work starts or incorporated with the core threads when working the cordonnette on the finished piece of lace, as preferred by Janet. Refer to pages 28-29 for instructions on laying a cordonnet and creating needlelace on a temporary foundation fabric.

The pin cushion

The pin cushions feature two further needlelace stitches, in addition to plain and spiral cordonnettes, and embroidered buttonhole wheels; a colour change on the cordonnettes adds further decoration.

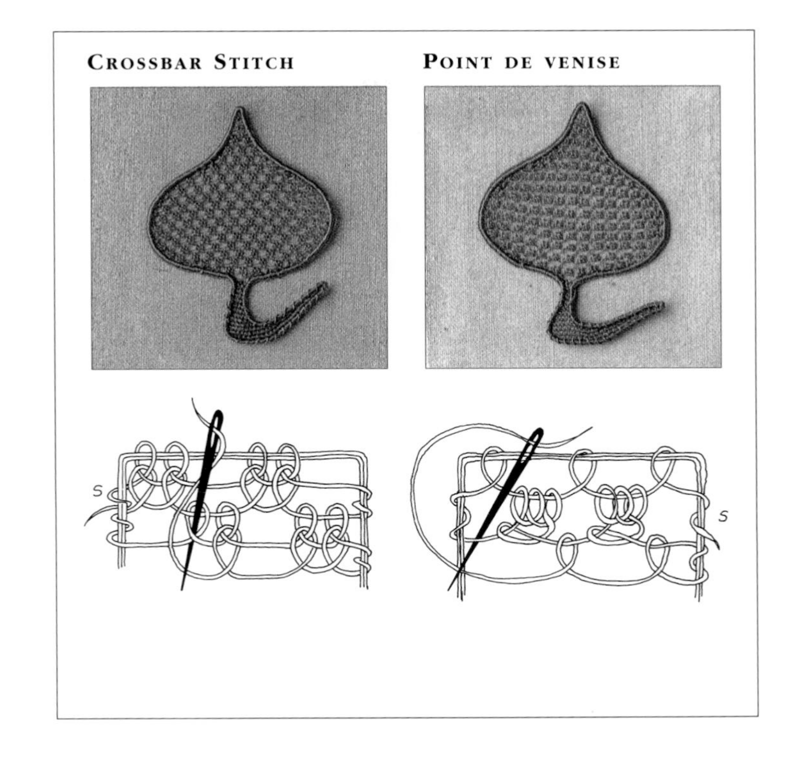

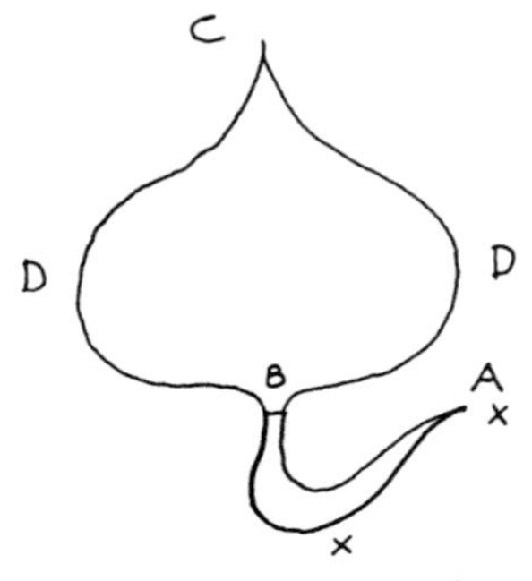

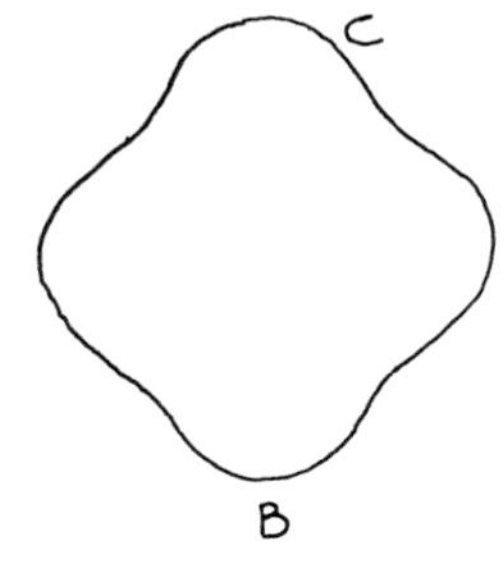

Start laying the leaf cordonnet at A. Fill the tail of each leaf with corded buttonhole stitch (page 28); work the first row from 'x' to 'x'. Fill two leaves and the centre piece in crossbar stitch (working from C down to B) and the remaining two leaves in a point de Venise variation (this time working from B to C). A beading wire plus four threads form the core for the final cordonnettes (plain around the leaf and spiral around the tail), which are worked before the needlelace is removed from its temporary foundation.

PLAIN CORDONNETTE

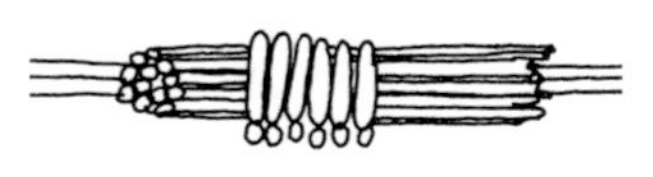

A cordonnette is a group of threads, of chosen thickness and number, buttonholed to the cordonnet on the finished needlelace edge. Start by anchoring the bundle of threads (plus a beading wire in selected cases) to the cordonnet with a few stitches; keep these taut while buttonhole stitching. The diagram shows the plain cordonnette.

SPIRAL CORDONNETTE

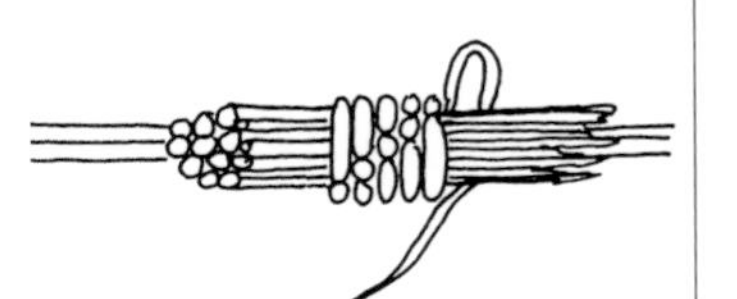

The spiral effect is achieved when the knot on each successive stitch is set higher than the last, so that they move from the bottom to the top of the cordonnette. Having reached the top, pass the needle behind the bundle and start again at the bottom.

CUSHION

The suggested working order is as follows:

* Stitch the central piece of needlelace to the ground (edge only) over a piece of felt of matching shape and colour; embroider a plentiful array of buttonhole wheels in varying sizes on the upper surface of the needlelace.
* Stitch two adjoining leaves to the ground between points B and D only; this allows the tail and the point of the leaf to 'fly in the air'.
* Cut the gold leather frame (page 66); firmly bond the backing paper and leave it permanently in position, and paint the raw leather edges with gold acrylic or fabric paint. Using a gold thread, attach the gold leather to the pin cushion with a couching stitch tight against each edge of the needlelace tail.
* Repeat the process with the remaining two leaves.

Chain Stitch

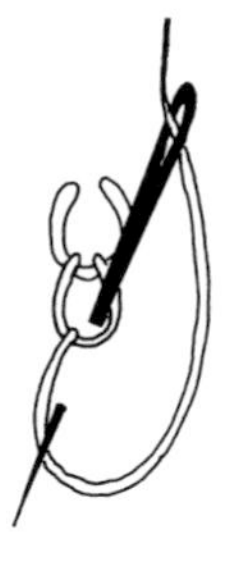

Pekin Knot

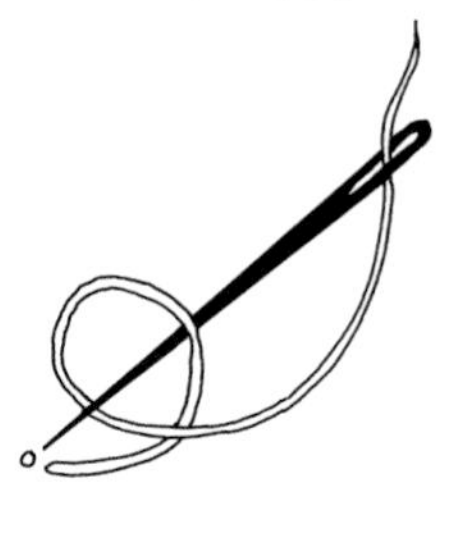

Stem Stitch

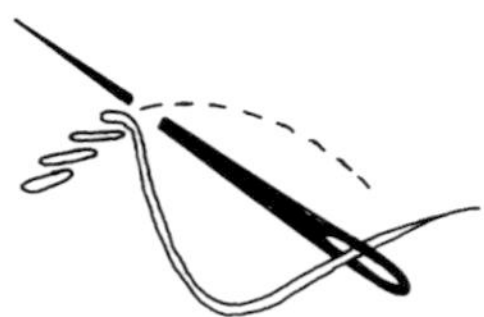

Buttonhole Wheels

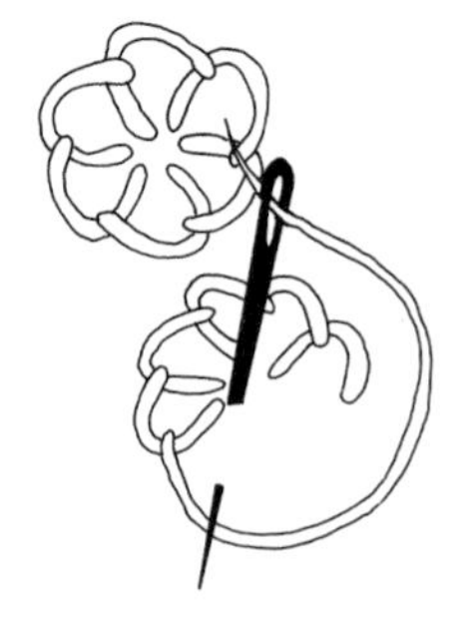

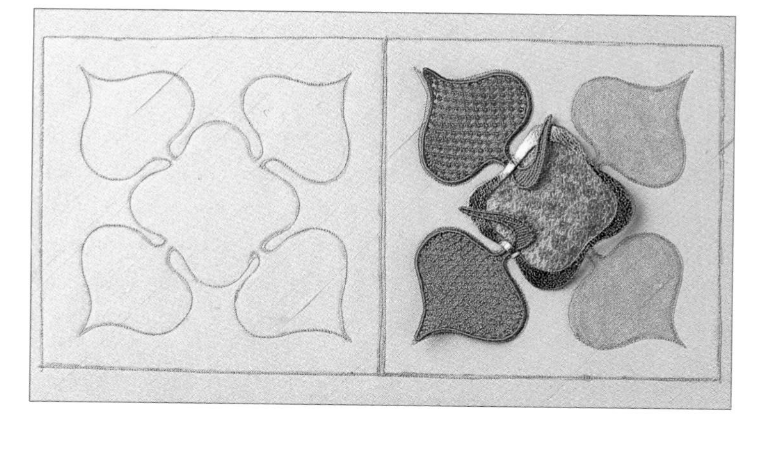

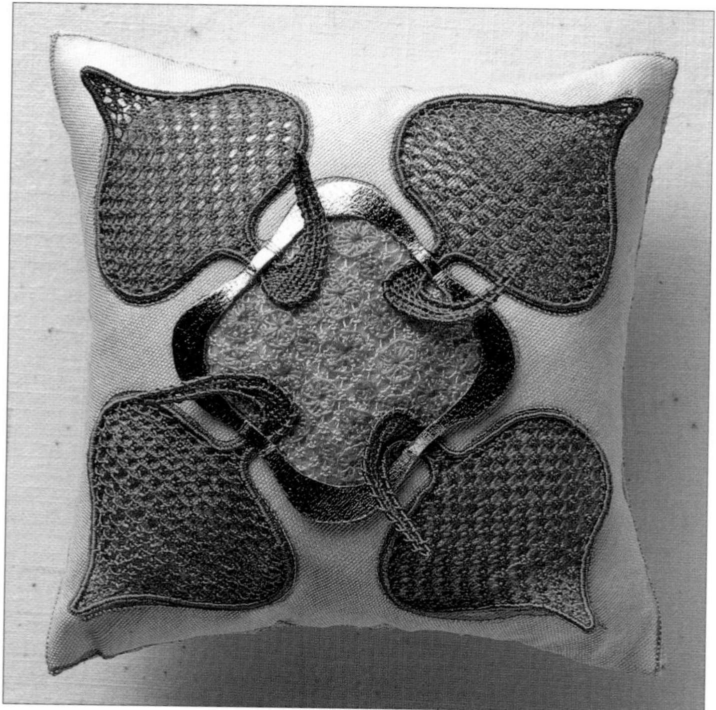

The finished art nouveau pin cushion.

NEEDLELACE FOR THE LARGE PEACOCK PURSE

Excluding the decorative roundels on the head and tail feathers, there are nine separate pieces of needlelace on the large purse, and each one is pricked out, or traced, from the design drawing. Remember to increase the size so that the needlelace can stretch over the padded shape and also overlap the piece of lace previously applied. Pieces 1, 3, and 5 have a duplicate mirror image.

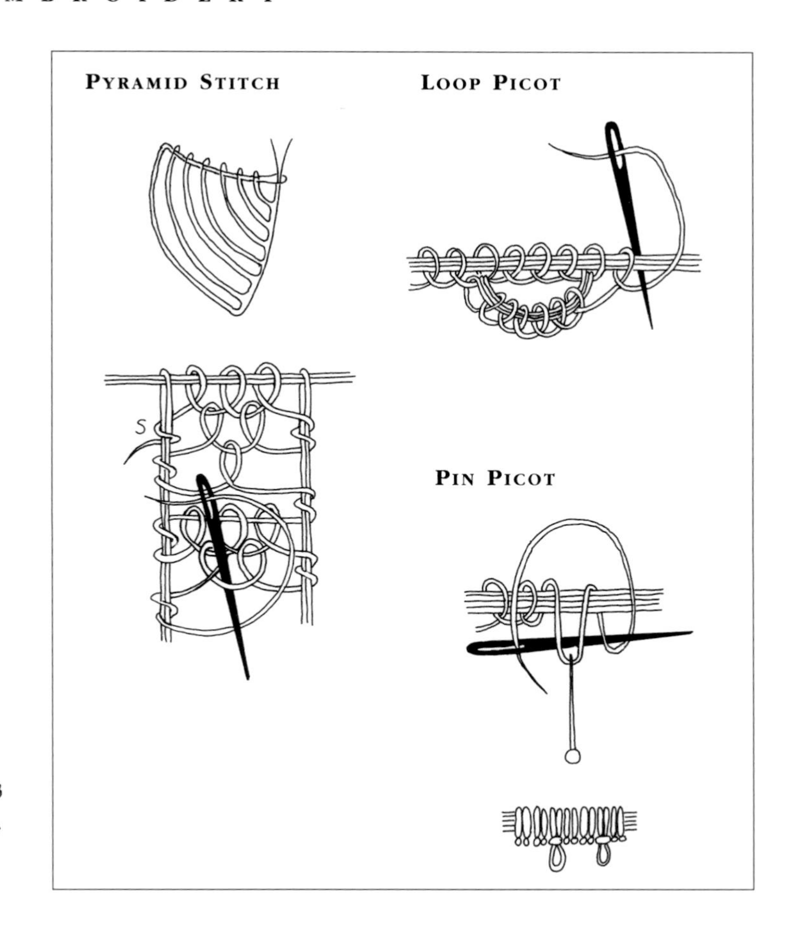

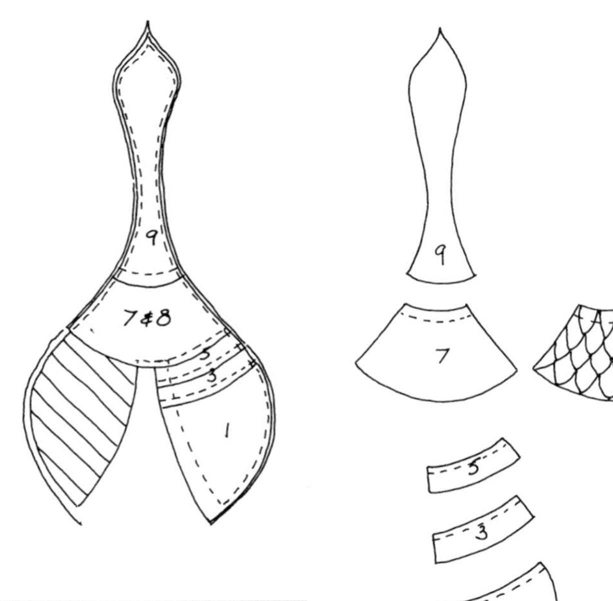

Completed needlelace pieces 1, 3 and 5

The suggested working order is as follows:

* Work 3, 5, 7, and 9 in corded buttonhole stitch. Add pin picots to the bottom edge of 7 and loop picots to the remainder.
* Shape 8 is worked in a lattice fashion. Refer to Henry VIII's waistcoat on page 29 and use similar methods.
* Lay the cordonnet for shape 1, then work pyramid stitch from top to bottom in the seven channels. The vein between each channel is buttonholed over using one thread and a beading wire in the core; the wire allows the wing to be domed. A cordonnette on the vertical inner edge has four decorative core threads; as the cordonnette is buttonholed, alternate colours of core thread are drawn out at regular intervals to form picots.
* The roundels on the head are worked as already described.

THE SMALL PURSE

The design drawings illustrate the front of the purse A, and the inner folding pouch B. In shape, the inner lining is a mirror image of A. The needlelace is worked in just two separate pieces, as illustrated, plus an added eye, worked as already described. Gold leather forms the beak, and the feather-stitch plumes are embroidered on the ground.

The suggested working order is as follows:

* Work the neck section on piece 1 in corded buttonhole stitch in coloured bands and complete the body section in lattice style.
* The head, piece 2, in single Brussels stitch, is worked round and round from the outer edge cordonnet, the colour changing from blue to green beneath the applied eye.

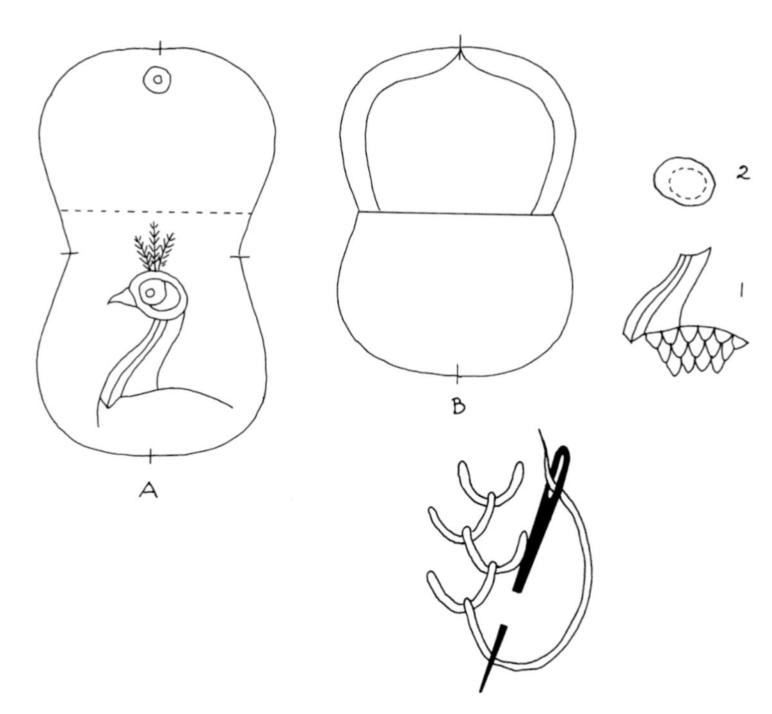

FEATHER STITCH

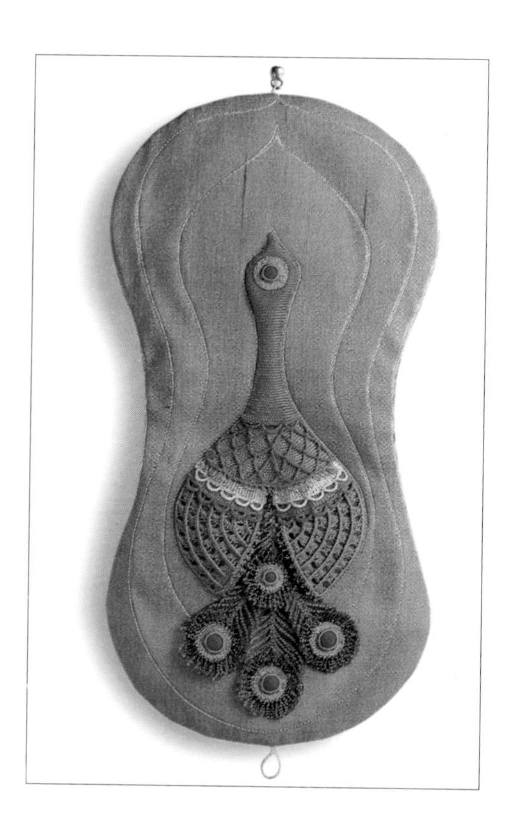

When all the needlelace and machine-embroidered tail feathers are complete, the pieces are applied over the padded shapes. Stitch the spine of each tail feather to the ground, then work progressively from the tail through to the head. Each piece of needlelace is carefully fitted and stitched in position within the machined gold outline on the ground fabric. Size: 22 x 11cm (8¾ x 4¾in), opened

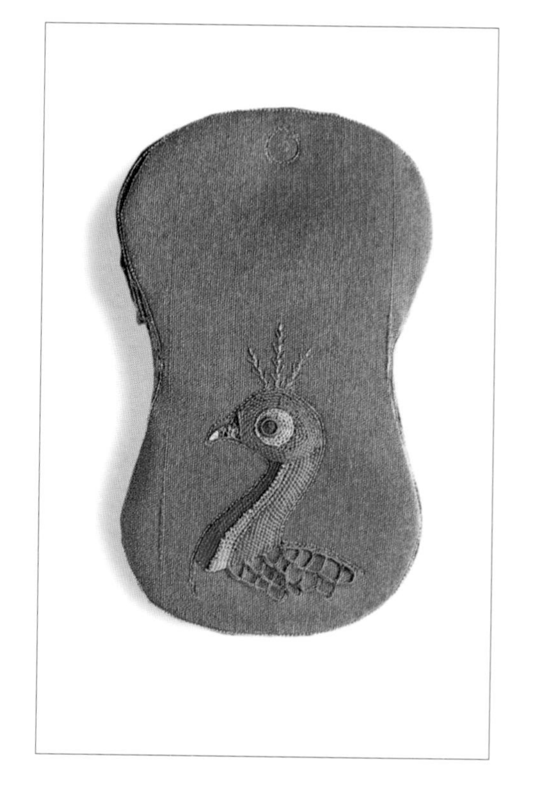

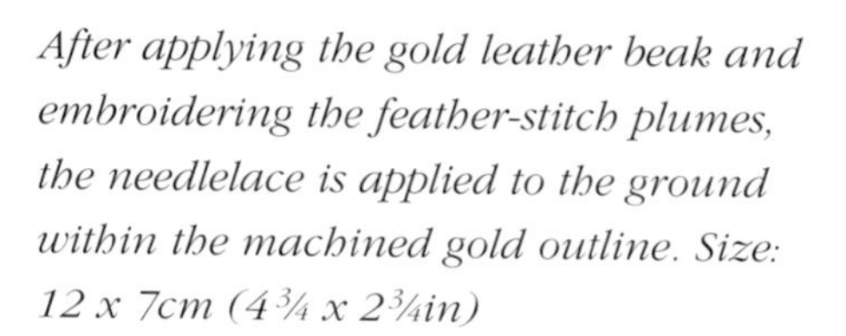

After applying the gold leather beak and embroidering the feather-stitch plumes, the needlelace is applied to the ground within the machined gold outline. Size: 12 x 7cm (4¾ x 2¾in)

ASSEMBLY GUIDE FOR PIN CUSHIONS AND PURSES

Baste a small piece of temporary protective fabric to the ground fabric, over the stumpwork, to prevent damage during assembly. Work in the described order and use matching strong threads when ladder stitching. The pad for the pin cushion, in white cotton or a similar fabric, should measure 11.5cm (4½in) square and be generously filled with loose polyester filling.

* Trim back the vilene close against the outer machine-stitched edge.
* Cut away the surplus ground fabric, leaving about 1cm (⅜in) outside the machine-stitched edge, for turning.
* First pin then baste the turning onto the vilene backing; snip as necessary at intervals around the curves, but avoid cutting too close to the machined edge.
* Herringbone stitch the turning to the vilene backing, ensuring that the metallic gold machine stitching is occurring on the edge of the piece of work. When completed, remove pins and basting threads.
* PURSES ONLY: machine stitch the back half of each pouch to the purse lining; fold the pouch in half, and ladder stitch the matching halves together, working between the two rows of metallic machine-edged stitching.
* PURSES ONLY: in their finished positions, baste the embroidered face to the purse lining, then ladder stitch these matching shapes together as described above.
* PIN CUSHION ONLY: fold the embroidered fabric in half, with faces outwards. Ladder stitch along two edges as described above; insert the prepared pad, and ladder stitch to close the final edge.

NOTE: use a curved needle when ladder stitching the corners of a box.

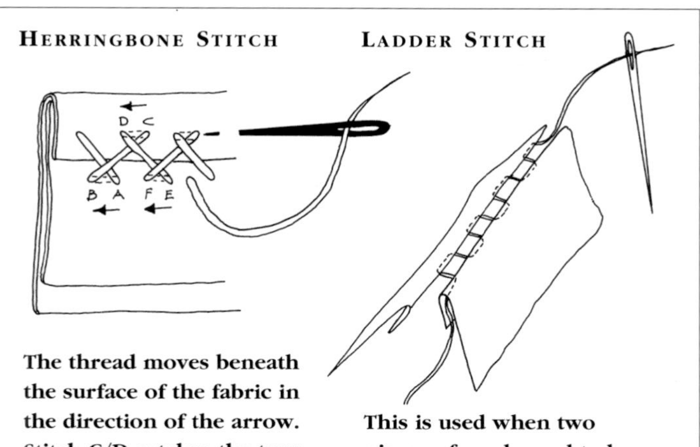

The thread moves beneath the surface of the fabric in the direction of the arrow. Stitch C/D catches the turning, while A/B and E/F catch the vilene backing. None of the stitches penetrate through to the face of the ground fabric. This stitching holds the turning firmly and permanently in position. The turning on the pouch for the large purse (below) has been herringbone stitched (in red).

This is used when two pieces of work need to be stitched together in an unobtrusive manner at a corner or edge. The pieces are separated in the illustration to show how the thread moves in short regular stitch lengths from one fabric to the other, crossing at right angles to ensure that it is completely hidden within the turning when it is pulled tight.

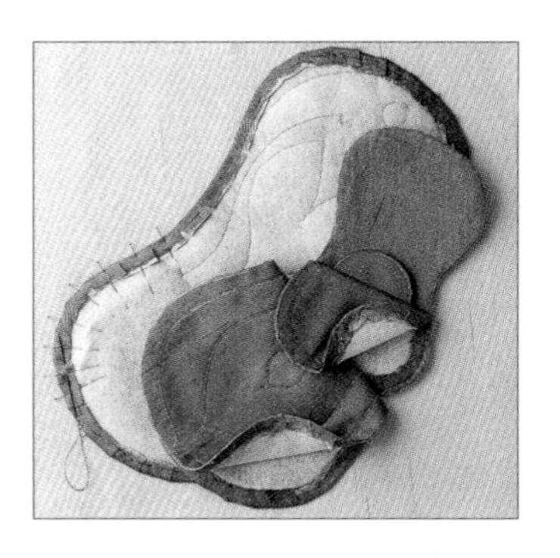

The back of the large purse lining shows the turning pinned and partly basted; the pouch for the small purse has been machined.

The inner lining, the raised embroidered face, and the two surfaces of the folded pouch are shown invisibly ladder-stitched together.

DECORATIVE ORNAMENTS

If we take the dictionary definition of ornament as that which adorns and embellishes, then Anne Smith's raised cockerel in needlelace on page 52, with the cordonnette core threads trailing from his tail feathers, admirably meets the definition. A similar raised cockerel can be created if these various illustrated shapes are worked in needlelace, with edge decorations, and applied to the ground fabric over a padded shape, as shown hatched on the right. Start by applying the tail feathers first, and ensure that each succeeding layer of needlelace overlaps the previous one; these rules apply whether you are working flat, in relief or in the round.

This kind of embossed work, covered in needlelace or embroidered slips, is the essence of 17th-century domestic raised embroidery, but occasionally the style becomes more exuberant and changes from work in relief to decorations completely in the round. When lifting the lid of a stumpwork casket of the 17th century, we can be surprised to find these free-standing decorations enjoying pride of place inside the box, demonstrating the imagination and dexterity of the embroiderer. These 3D objects were usually worked in needlelace over boxwood moulds; today, we might prefer to work the needlelace over spun cotton balls or a shape made from soft balsawood.

Needlelace in the Round

Stitch a number of anchoring threads over the mould, passing through a hole or holes and intersecting at some point. The starting point for the needlelace is provided by two winds of thread passing under the anchoring threads at their point of intersection. Buttonhole over the double threads, and then continue to buttonhole around and around the mould, gradually increasing or decreasing the number of stitches as necessary and occasionally linking to the anchoring threads as work proceeds. Insert a doubled beading wire through the central hole and buttonhole over this to form a stem.

A balsawood mould can be whittled from a square section obtainable at a modelling shop. It is then smoothed with sandpaper; drilled to provide holes for anchoring threads; coloured with acrylic paints, fabric paints or dyes to match the thread colours, and even varnished if a shine is required. This body mould for a bird is similar to the one made for the *Exotic Bird*, and with a little ingenuity it can be covered in needlelace; this in turn supports all the other wire-edged pieces of needlelace that ultimately create the sculptured ornament.

Orange Tree with Guarding Sheep *by Anne Smith – both this and the cockerel on page 52 are details from a larger sampler. Size (this section only): 13 x 6.5cm (5 x 2½in)*

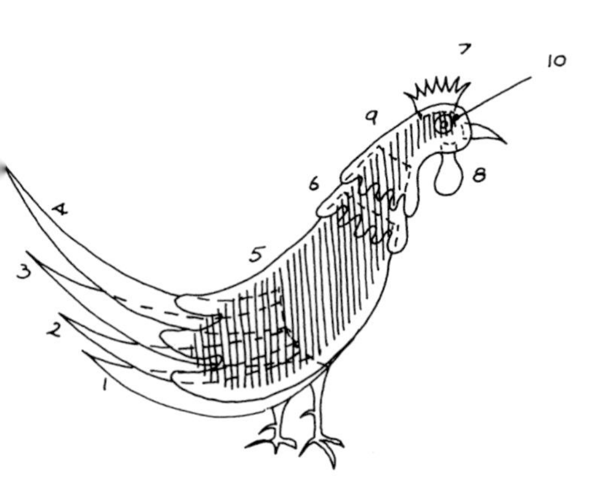

Design for a raised cockerel in needlelace. Apply each piece in the numbered order.

DESIGN DRAWING FOR SCULPTURED BIRD

Work the sixteen shapes (below right) in chosen needlelace stitches, reserving the most elaborate stitches for the tail and back. Decorate the edges with pin or loop picots, or draw out the threads in little tufts from the core of the cordonnette. Add other decorations to the surfaces of the lace. Beading wire must be added to the edges of all the larger pieces of needlelace in order that they can be manipulated into, and subsequently retain the necessary sculptural form.

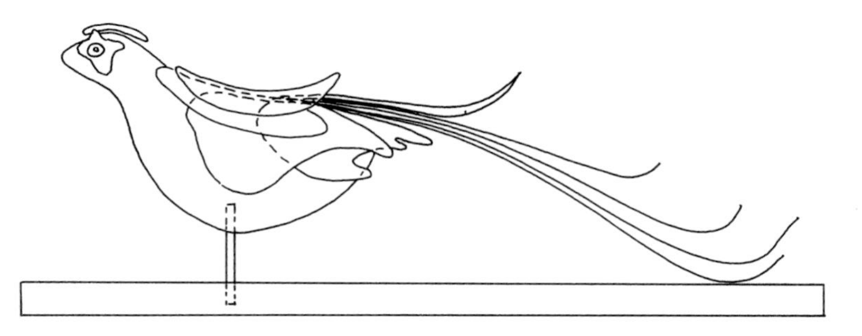

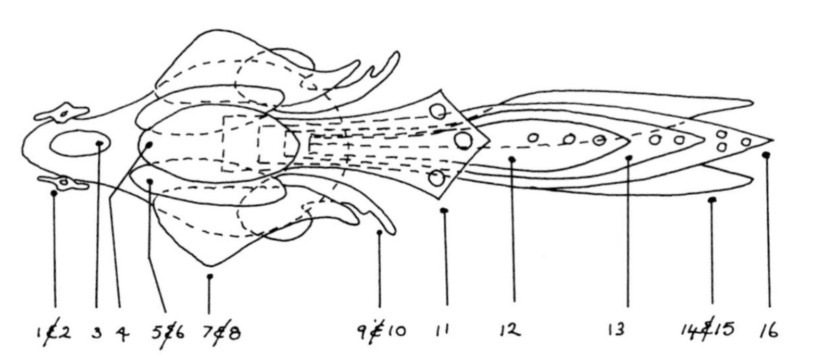

The sculptured, free standing Exotic Bird *has silk-wrapped wire legs that raise the body from the base, bullion-knot feet worked on the ground, and a balsawood body, covered in needlelace, which in turn supports sixteen, mostly wire-edged, needlelace pieces. The head decorations, wings and tail feathers, in single and corded Brussels stitches, have additional picot decorations and applied couronnes with picot edges.*
Size: 18 x 4.5 x 6cm (7 x 1¾ x 2¼in)

CHAPTER FIVE

BOXES, MIRROR FRAMES & BOOK COVERS

At the peak of her embroidery skills, having consumed both time and patience on practising stitches and techniques, working samplers, and perhaps some simple pictorial embroideries, the 17th-century domestic embroiderer finally achieves her ambition and completes an important constructional piece of stumpwork which is destined to become a highly treasured family possession. These constructional 17th-century pieces come in a limited range of shapes and designs, and it is probable that individual craftsmen would have made their skills available to the contemporary domestic embroiderer at the appropriate stages, including the creation of the embroidery patterns, their transfer to fabric, the fashioning of the wooden boxes, caskets and frames, and finally mounting the finished embroideries on their wooden bases.

A 17th-century casket can easily comprise 25, or more, separate pieces of embroidery, and it would be commenced only after much forethought. If it was to be the work of a girl, one can imagine endless preliminary discussions between parents and governess and, ultimately, the excitement when designs and materials were chosen. In spite of all the preparation and planning, and for the many reasons which embroiderers well understand, some embroideries were, fortunately, never completed, and a number of these are safely preserved and have become valuable visual aids today.

Our designs and work style for the mirror frame *Baroque Reflections* and the *Tristram Box* owe much to this heritage, while also incorporating 20th-century methods and techniques. The *Tristram Box* is of course modest when compared with its historical counterpart. The designs and working methods provided can be faithfully followed, but we trust that some embroiderers will vary these to meet their own inclinations or be inspired to break new ground with their own designs and techniques.

This embroidered jewellery casket features the story of Isaac and Rebecca as its main theme. As an additional delight, there is a miniature wax effigy of a lady within the lid. Size: 35 x 25 x 32cm (14 x 10 x 12⅝in); gift of Mrs Elizabeth Learned Peabody, Courtesy of the Museum of Fine Arts, Boston, USA.

The ivory satin ground of this mirror frame, featuring incidents from the life of Abraham, illustrates the 17th-century method of drawing outlines in ink. In 1896 the Victoria and Albert Museum, London, purchased this unfinished treasure for £8. Photographed by Daniel McGrath. Size: 70 x 56cm (28 x 22in)

THE TRISTRAM BOX

The sea is the linking design theme for this simple rectangular box. In raised embroidery, it has shell-like feet; mermaids and fish on the sides, providing a link with 17th-century designs, and on the lid a king-like figure blowing a boatswain's whistle and beating time for a group of soldier oarsmen, a scene inspired by a similar design on the *Tristram Quilt*.

Some of these raised images could well be carried through onto the inner faces of the box in stumpwork embroidery, but in our example we have worked simple dolphin shapes and margin lines in machine quilting. The decorative machine stitching that edges the outer panels simulates the braids which the 17th-century cabinet maker glued and nailed to boxes and panels to mask raw fabric edges.

Because of its strength and non-stretch qualities, unbleached and unwashed calico was chosen for the ground fabric and in a medium weight only, to avoid excess bulk when mounting the embroidery on the card base. Silk dyes in colours reminiscent of the sea, sky, sand and shells were applied to the moist ground fabric and encouraged to coalesce freely. The machine-embroidered slips for sea and boat are worked on blue/green and bronze silk organza, and the chosen threads include silk and rayon, as well as smooth metallic machine threads in silver, gold, bronze, and multicolours. Some of the embroidered slips are backed with iron-on vilene.

The completed box has six external faces, each with raised embroidery, and six embroidered linings. Size: 17.5 x 13.5 x 9.5cm (7 x 5¼ x 3⅜in)

From the outset, it is essential to ensure that you have sufficient materials to complete the project. Work with the ground fabrics stretched taut in a round embroidery frame throughout the hand embroidery process; this will avoid problems when the work is finally stretched.

MAKING A START

Enlarge the six design drawings to the required size. Following enlargement, check that the designs for the lid and sides still match lengthways and widthways. A separate design for the bottom is unnecessary; simply use the edge design for the lid.

Having dyed the twelve ground fabrics (six outer pieces plus six linings), use gold fabric paint to add the following: an indication of the position of each added slip (sea, boat, flag, mermaids and fish); the four parallel equally-spaced lines around the lid and bottom, and along the top and bottom edges of the side panels; the similar single lines, and fish, on the linings, and the complete outlines of those figures on the lid that are to be worked directly onto the ground. Remember to keep all gold lines for stumpwork images inside the lines on the design drawing, and do not define hands, hair or the fins on the fish because these are flying 'in the air'.

Back the linings with felt to achieve a quilting effect when machine stitching.

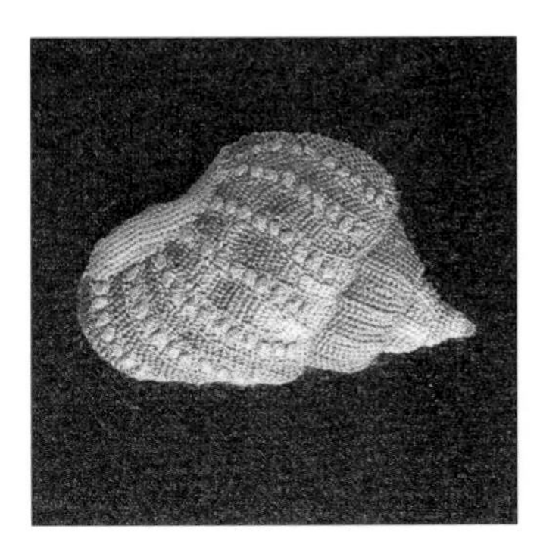

Stumpwork needlelace shells, similar to this example worked by Janet Taff, would make excellent feet for a box.

Simulated Braids

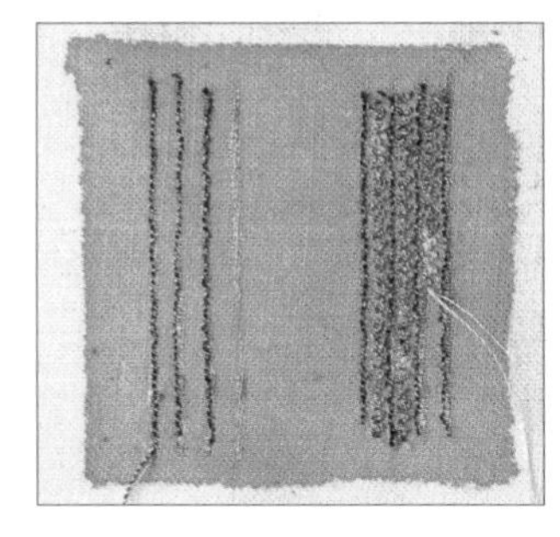

With the machine in normal stitching mode, overlay the four painted gold lines with a straight stitch, then fill the three channels with a chosen fancy stitch. To achieve the braid-like quality, experiment with a multi-coloured rayon bobbin thread, varied thread tensions, and a gold, bronze, or multi-coloured metallic top thread.

Shell Feet

Each foot has three components: a shell-shaped card base, over which are placed a few felt layers in reducing sizes, and a dyed/painted and machine-stitched lightweight calico slip. The slip is stretched over the padded card, and the calico margins are bonded to the underside of the card. Metallic white pearl fabric paint, applied over the dye, adds the shell-like sheen. A few stitches attach the foot to the ground fabric while it is still in its round embroidery frame.

BOTTOM LAYERS OF THE CONSTRUCTION

The tissue paper pattern technique (page 36, Machine embroidered decorations) is used when making the various machined slips. For accurate shapes, use the machine in normal stitching mode, repetitively lifting and dropping the presser foot and pivoting the fabric on the needle in the process. Singe the edges of the organza slips and seal the remainder with acrylic paint.

Design drawings of box side and end: the mermaids on the ends of the box are mirror images of each other; the front and back are identical.

CONSTRUCTING THE SIDES

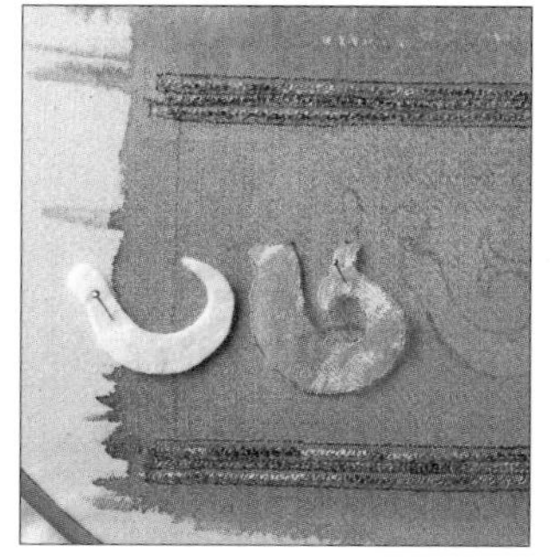

1 Gold outlines, sufficient to define the position of the mermaid, sea, and mirror, have been transferred to the ground; a colourless transparent slip, with a machine-embroidered edge, and a white felt shape (left) have been prepared and are ready for attaching, in that order, on top of the lowest 'sea' slip. Soft filling will be inserted beneath the felt. To be visible, the transparent fish slip needs to be a little larger than the image on the design drawing.

2 The 'sea' slips are created on blue/green silk organza with a number of added wavy machine-stitched lines. A turquoise bobbin thread is used in combination with a metallic silver machine thread. Loosely stitch the sea slip to the ground; follow by attaching the fish shapes, allowing the fins to fly free. Apply the felt, and insert soft filling material. These design features also occur on the lid beneath the boat. Emphasize the top edge of the sea slip with satin stitch. Apply the mermaids' heads or create them directly on the ground at this stage (see page 34), but wait until the body slip has been attached before stitching the hair.

3 The seaweed, mirror, comb, collar and waistband, in free machine embroidery, will provide embellishments to be added later to the hand-embroidered slips covering the padded bodies of the fish and mermaids. Using a dark green silk organza, work in a round embroidery frame over a tracing of the required shapes; cut away surplus organza and singe the edges on completion. The mirror has two layers of organza. Machine stitch the top layer, then cut away and singe, including the central hole. Anchor the small top image to a lower layer of organza, sandwiching the small piece of mica (or acetate film) between the two; machine the small image to the bottom layer, then cut away the edges and singe again to complete the small artefact.

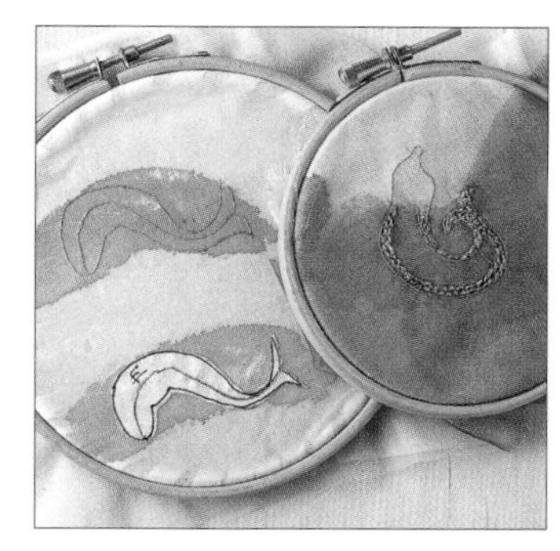

4 The hand-embroidered slips for mermaids and fish are prepared separately on an upper layer of pale blue or cream silk organza and a composite ground of lightweight vilene, dyed with silk dyes. Machine stitch around the edge of each image and along the centre line of the fish, using the same methods as before. Now fill the chosen area of each image with a hand embroidery stitch; buttonhole stitches (in a multi-coloured metallic machine thread) suspended on rows of back stitches, in a turquoise rayon machine thread, are illustrated (page 13). When the hand stitching is complete, cut away the surplus ground fabric, leaving about 2mm ($^1/_{12}$in) outside the machine stitched edge. Firmly, but with care, stitch the slip over the padded shapes on the ground fabric. Now stitch the hair over the mermaid's head.

5 To complete the box sides, fashion a further blue or blue/green machined sea slip to represent the foreground sea. This should be narrower than the back one, but have a common shape on both top and bottom edges. Machine stitch the slip to the ground along the bottom edge, and lightly hand stitch the top in one or two selected places. Lightly hand stitch the seaweed slips in position in order to break the bottom edge of the sea. Add the mermaids' combs, waist bands and mirrors.

THE TRISTRAM LID

The seven figures wear needlelace in corded buttonhole stitch. The T-shaped turquoise body, worked in one piece, is applied over felt and soft filling; gold straight stitches form the lattice pattern. Each soldier is padded with one layer of felt beneath the needlelace body; further relief is achieved with the wire arm, which is covered with felt and needlelace. Complete the front soldier first, then follow with each one in turn. The slip for the machine-embroidered boat, in dyed vilene covered with a bronze silk organza, has a machine-stitched edge and further decorative stitching; the edges are sealed with acrylic paint.Suggest rythmic movement by placing hands, arms and oars repetitively.

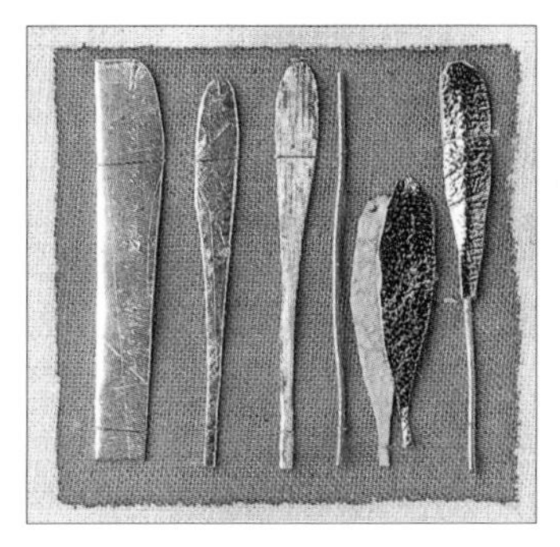

1 The oars are either cut from aluminium and filed to shape or formed with a piece of wire bonded between two pieces of leather. Paint the metal and the leather edges in gold.

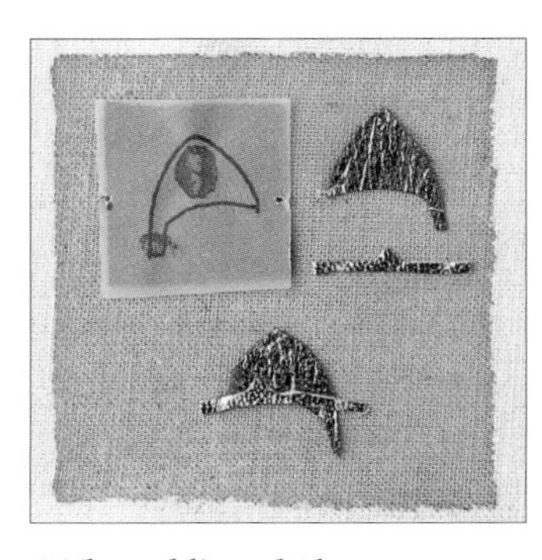

2 The soldiers' helmets are formed from two pieces of leather bonded together. A tracing bonded to the leather back serves as a cutting guide and also stiffens the leather. The edge of the paper is cut away to permit stitching.

3 Apply the bottom layers of the lid in this order: first, the brown shadow of the boat; second, the seven figures through to completion; third, the blue/green sea slip, and finally, the flag and staff. Each soldier, wearing chain-mail and doublet, is clad in just four pieces of needlelace, as illustrated (below left).

4 When all the figures are complete, the boat slip can be machine-stitched to the ground; leave the top edge free. Fix each oar to a soldier's hand and then create a fixing loop (a rowlock) on the top edge of the boat. Keep the oars parallel with one another.

NEEDLELACE SHAPES

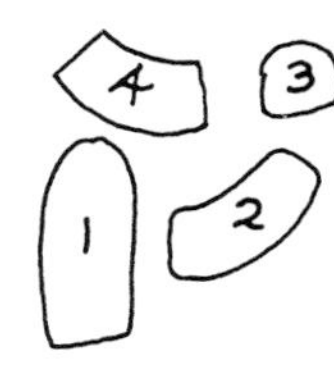

Apply 1 (doublet), 2 (chain-mail sleeve), 3 (short doublet sleeve), and 4 (chain mail collar) in this order.

5 In the manner previously described, apply the narrower foreground sea slip and then the seaweed. The needlelace turban head-dress worn by the kingly figure has radiating metallic gold stitches to give shape and style.

BOX ASSEMBLY GUIDE

Baste a small piece of temporary protective fabric over the stumpwork to prevent damage during assembly. Work in the described order and use matching threads for ladder stitching.

*Using cardboard about 3mm (⅛in) thick, accurately measure and cut the six rectangles required for lid and bottom, two sides and two ends. Cut these in matching pairs. Where corners meet, cut the card with the edges at a 45 degree angle so that the sides will mitre comfortably together.

*Bond felt (using white glue) to the outer surfaces of each card; this will soften the surfaces and corners of the box.

*Stretch and lace the bottom and four sides to the matching cards as described on page 19. Start with the box bottom, and check the card size for each side before stretching and lacing the side embroideries.

*Ladder stitch the fabrics at the edges where the bottom meets the sides, and on the four vertical corners. Start by attaching the bottom edges of the back and one side, then proceed to ladder stitch the first corner.

*Check the card size for the lid before stretching and lacing the embroidery. Firmly bond and stitch tape hinges and a stay to the inside surface of the lid before ladder stitching the lid to the back edge of the box. Dye the tapes to match the box colours. Bond and stitch the hinges and stay to the vertical inside faces of the box.

*Stretch and lace the six inside linings over card (use thinner card for lining sections) and bond each finished piece to an inside face of the box. Fit each card separately before stretching and lacing the fabric; if backing felt has been used, cut this back to match the card size. Avoid excessively tight fits which distort the ladder stitching on the outer corners of the box. Start with the bottom; follow with the four sides, keeping these about 6mm (¼in) lower than the outer sides. The fabric-covered card for the lid lining needs to fit easily within the top of the box (resting on top of the side linings) before being firmly bonded to the inside of the lid. Trap a tape finger grip, for opening the box, between lid and lining.

The inside linings are ready to be fixed inside the box.

The tape hinges can clearly be seen here. They will be covered when the linings are fixed inside the box.

BAROQUE REFLECTIONS
A MIRROR FRAME

We chose the baroque period for the mirror frame because of the way it encourages an unlimited abundance of decoration, rich fabric surfaces, elaborate costumed figures, and an overall exuberance and extravagance in colour and design.

The strong unbleached and unwashed calico of the main ground fabric receives the painted gold-outlined design and the warm brush-dyed colours, which occasionally echo the colours of the instruments or costume, or a candlelit interior, or the clouds in the sky which shelter angels. To add richness and sheen, a warm nut-brown silk organza overlays the dyed calico, and the two are freely machined together in vermicelli stitch, which occasionally merges with musical images. Fragments of music are also trapped between the two fabrics as a further elaboration.

The ground for a 17th-century mirror frame would have been stretched in a fairly large rectangular embroidery frame. A smaller frame is easier for machine embroiderers, so *Baroque Reflections* is embroidered in six separate pieces, each small enough to fit a frame 30cm (12in) in diameter.

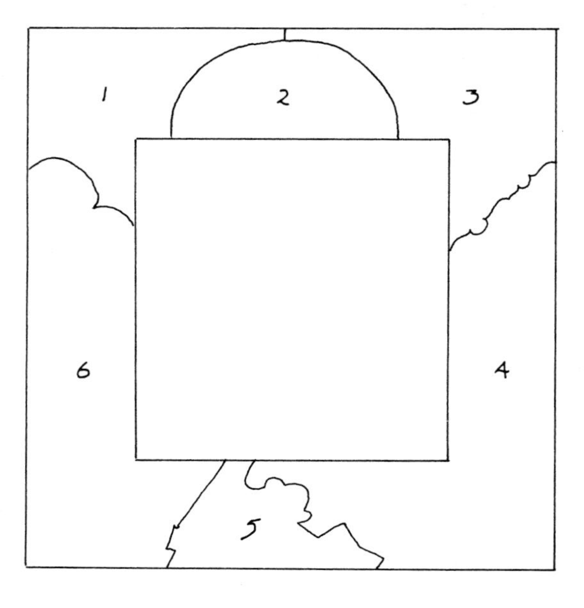

The Six Embroideries
The above drawing illustrates the division of the embroidery into its six separate parts, the design having been devised to make this possible. During construction, the parts overlap each other and are machine stitched together after being fitted to the base frame.

A full-size colour cartoon on paper (like this one, seen on the left) is a worthwhile undertaking, providing early impressions of the finished embroidery. It assists when making colour choices for dyes, threads, and fabrics, and continues to be useful as the design takes shape on fabric.

Baroque Reflections *is a mirror frame in the 17th-century mode, relying on its many images to create an overall design. Size: 34cm (13½ in) square*

THE MIRROR FRAME BASE

For simplicity in construction, the base is cut from medium density fibreboard (MDF) not less than 1cm (3/8in) thick. A standard mirror tile 23cm (9in) square is housed in a shallow MDF box, which is screwed to the back of the mirror frame. The material is sufficiently strong to receive fixing screws and hooks or other hanging equipment. The MDF frame and the design drawing are identical in size.

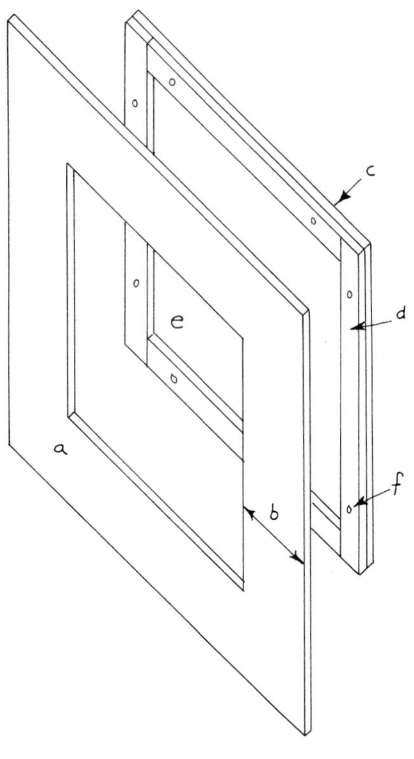

The Design Drawing
This design drawing is much reduced in size; it should be enlarged to 34cm (13½in) square before transferring the designs to fabric.

As each of the six pieces of embroidery is completed, it can be trimmed to size, fitted to the frame, and temporarily attached to the frame with drawing pins. Leave a turning of about 4cm (1½in) beyond the machine-stitched edges. When all six completed embroideries have been dealt with in this manner, as well as being fitted and pinned or basted to each other, they can be machine stitched together. The composite embroidery can now be stretched and laced to the MDF frame in much the same manner as a simple panel, but with the lacing sometimes restricted to one direction only on the narrow frame edges.

Fitting the Embroideries

Finished embroidery sections 5 and 6 have been fitted and temporarily pinned to the frame. The left- and right-hand edges of section 5 have been trimmed to the design shape; the main calico ground is cut back to the machine-stitched edges, while the top organza is allowed to extend by 3mm (⅛in) and singed to prevent fraying. The top, overlapping edges of sections 4 and 6, the curved edge of section 2, and the bottom edges of the clouds are all given this design feature.

Artefacts and Decorative Materials

In addition to the silk organza, other decorative and metallic materials can be used to create waistcoats, angels' wings and bodies, music stands, instruments, and the trim around the mirror.

The entire frame (a) measures 34cm (13½in) square; the width of the frame sections (b) is 7cm (2¾in); the back for the box (c) measures 28cm (11in) square; the small wood fillets (d), measuring about 2.5cm x 1cm (1 x ⅜in) are glued and pinned to the box back; the shallow well (e) receives the 23cm (9in) square mirror tile, and the box is screwed to the frame through the holes (f).

COLOUR AND DESIGN

Transfer the design to the calico ground; the lines should be bold, as the organza masks the gold colour and they can be difficult to see while working. The colours in the lower parts of the frame are deep and warm; towards the top they fade, giving way to shades of blue on the clouds.

All six embroideries are edged with a machined metallic gold thread in straight stitches; this also attaches the organza to the calico ground. The design on the overlapping edges of the six embroideries is emphasized in satin stitch (zigzag).

A pale gold rayon bobbin thread is used continuously, but the top thread changes according to design needs; deep rich rose is the predominant colour, but in small areas, adjacent to the figures and on the clouds, blues, turquoise and green are introduced. Thread tensions are varied to ensure that the pale gold rayon bobbin thread whips on the surface of the embroidery, the effect increasing gradually to a more marked extent at the top of the frame. Special details are picked out in the gold metallic machine thread. Pin or baste the silk organza to the calico ground; keep the fabrics taut in a round embroidery frame throughout, but change from free machine to normal mode at the appropriate stages; leave a 1cm (⅜in) turning of silk organza beyond the finished outer edges of the mirror frame, and machine this to the calico ground before attempting to stretch and lace the embroidery to the base frame.

DYES AND SILK ORGANZA

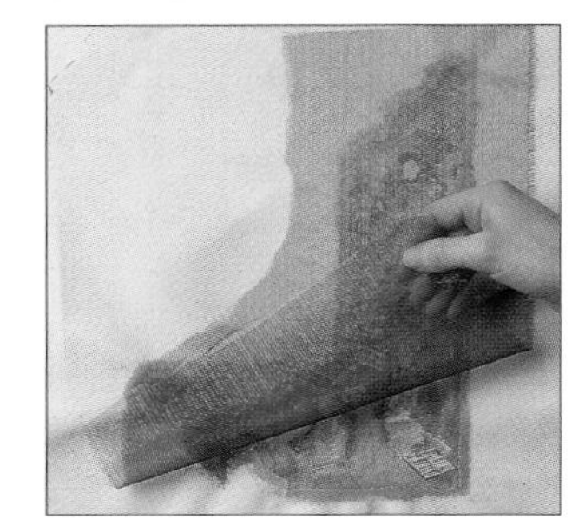

The dyes are applied as previously described for the *Tristram Box*. Take into account the colour change that will occur when the organza layer is added. Experiment before dyeing all six ground fabrics in one operation.

LOOKING AHEAD

The vermicelli stitching will again change the surface colour of the embroidery. Carry out stitch experiments on samples of the dyed composite ground before finally stitching the six embroideries with selected threads.

Vermicelli Stitch

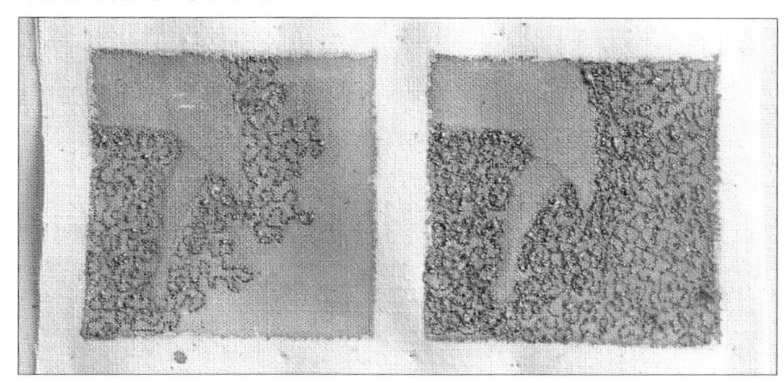

In its pure form, the continuously reversing half circles which create the stitch will never overlap each other. On the mirror frame, two separately-stitched layers of vermicelli, in two different colours, overlay each other in the vicinity of each male musician. A blue, green or turquoise top thread is used in the bottom layer in close proximity to the figure (see left). The warm deep rose is used for the upper layer and for the whole frame (see right). The organza is omitted for clarity.

The Conductor's Head

Make and stitch in position the padded oval head slip (omitting facial features); cover with a felt oval; densely cover the felt with satin stitches; bring many separate threads through the ground (each one knotted) along the top edges of the head; fold these down over the head and anchor them with couching stitches at the nape of the neck; now separate the threads into three groups and form a plait; anchor the plait near the bottom and attach a tiny needlelace bow.

Wind Instruments

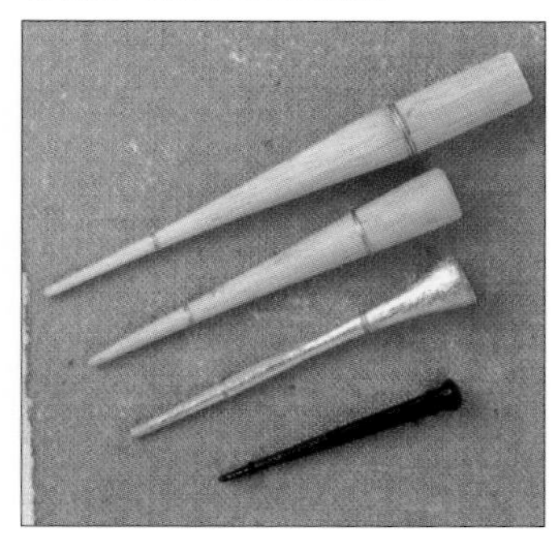

Use 3mm (⅛in) and 6mm (¼in) wooden dowels. Whittle the instruments to shape on the end of a piece of dowel (so that you can hold it comfortably, the dowel must be longer than the finished instrument). Smooth the whittled shape with a file and sandpaper. Using a very fine saw, cut the instrument from the length of dowel; smooth the cut end, and paint appropriately.

Clouds

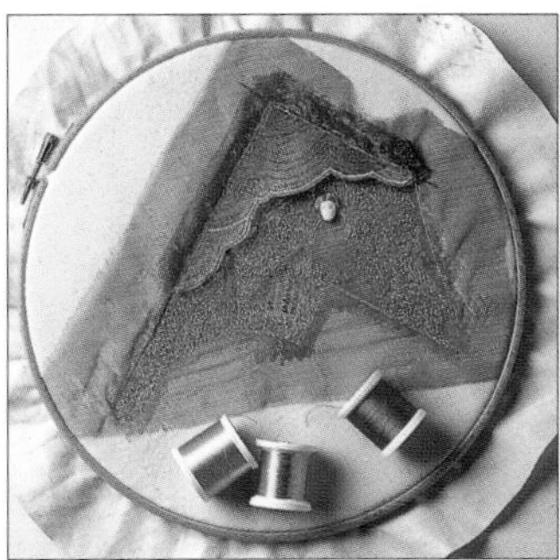

These are worked as separate slips on a dyed medium-weight vilene, overlayed with the nut-brown organza. Cut the vilene back to the machine-stitched edges before machining the slip to the main ground fabric on the two outer edges only. Singe the bottom edge. Stitch the organza turnings to the calico beyond the mirror frame edges. The deep rose, pale gold and metallic gold threads are illustrated as a colour guide for the frame in general.

ANGEL MUSICIANS

The angels are inspired by Evelyn de Morgan's *Angel Trumpeters* and a detail from the *Bedford Hours* of 1423. They are not padded in a traditional stumpwork manner but are simply built up in a series of machine-stitched slips, worked either on silk organza (finished with singed edges) or on a gold or bronze metallic fabric, finished with acrylic paint on the edge. The silk-wrapped wire arms, inserted beneath one of the layers, raise the slips above the ground fabric. A twisted gold cord couched along the top edge of the final layer adds essential decoration and finish. The shape of each slip is illustrated below; correct the size of these diagrams to match the enlarged design drawing. Apply the slips loosely, and with some sensitivity, to the ground fabric, and work in the order described.

ANGEL TRUMPETER

Work the head directly on the ground or make it separately and apply it. Do not stitch the hair. Apply slip 1 to the ground. Firmly stitch the arm to the ground, then apply slips 2 and 3 in that order. Couch the twisted gold braid in position. Complete the hair in long straight stitches, and then firmly fix the trumpet to the hand and ground.

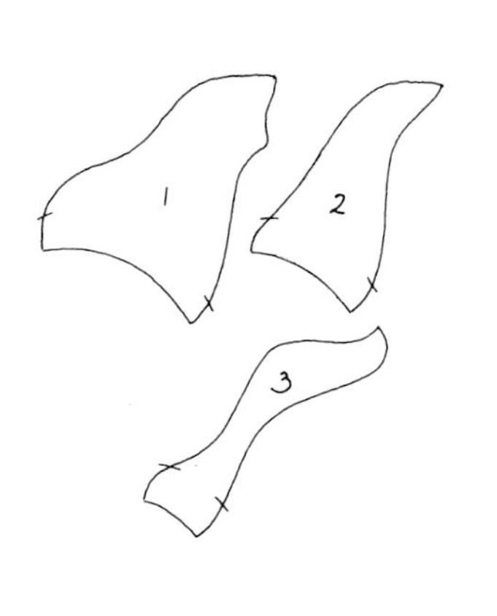

ANGEL VIOLINIST

Work the head directly on the ground or make it separately and apply it. Complete the hair style. Slip 1, cut from a clear transparent fabric and without a machine-stitched edge, is stitched to the ground beneath slip 2, which is now also applied. Firmly stitch the angel's left arm to the ground beneath slip 3, which is now also applied. Firmly stitch the second arm in position. Apply slip 4 over it, and then slip 5, and finish by couching the twisted gold braid. Firmly stitch the violin and bow in position. See page 46.

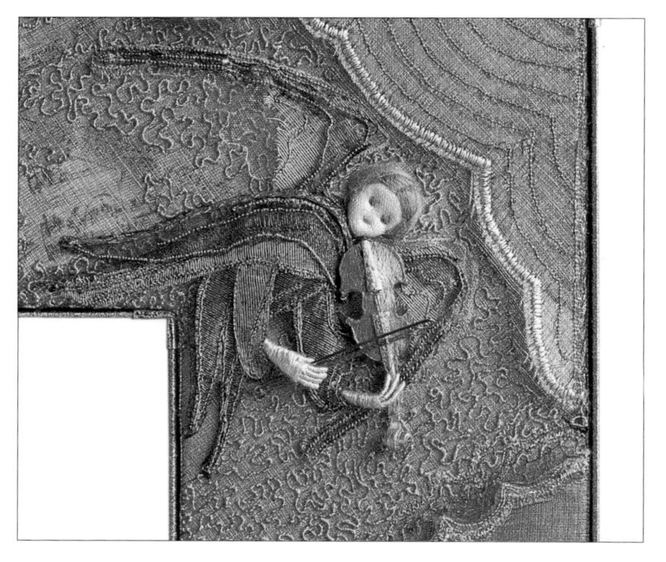

STUMPWORK BOOK COVERS

Almost impossible to handle, or lay flat without inflicting damage or wear, it is difficult to imagine anything less practical than raised embroidery on the cover of a book. Nevertheless, numerous 17th-century examples still exist today, demonstrating the popularity of this decorative art form three and a half centuries ago, and also showing that such items are perhaps less vulnerable than one might at first think.

THE CISTERCIAN MONKS

Originally worked and mounted as small panels (26cm square), our *Cistercian Reaper* and *Baker* were given new homes in 1994 when they were set into the covers of this leather-bound copy of *Raised Embroidery – a Practical Guide to Decorative Stumpwork*. For added protection, the book rests in a padded and velvet-lined case. The binding, in blue goatskin with blind tooling, is by Elizabeth Young (Benn). The embroideries have dyed and machine-stitched grounds and raised embroidered centres, inspired by the roundels in mediaeval manuscripts. Whether impractical or not, this is perhaps a fitting reminder that raised embroidery continues to fascinate the 20th-century embroiderer.

LIST OF STUMPWORK COLLECTIONS

This selected information is abbreviated and confined to the following headings in the listed order: museum reference; dimensions to nearest centimetre; type – P = panel, B = box/casket, M = mirror frame, C = cushion, Bk = book cover, and main design subject, with working dates and initials where known.

Birmingham, Museum and Art Gallery

Reference	Dimensions	Type	Subject
M6'45	17 x 11 x 4	Bk	Virtues
1887 Loan	42 x 42	P	Abraham offering Isaac
7'61 Loan	52 x 53	P	Judgement of Solomon
*	38 x 26	P	Adam and Eve

The Bowes Museum, Barnard Castle

Reference	Dimensions	Type	Subject
Emb. 375	41 x 26	P	Seated woman/cornucopia
Emb. 570	40 x 33	P	Man and two women/arbor
Emb. 2.50	27 x 20	P	Jephtha and his daughter
ditto	27 x 15	P	Solomon/Queen of Sheba

Bristol, Museum and Art Gallery

Reference	Dimensions	Type	Subject
NN	28 x 23 x 19	B	Judith and Holofernes/ allegorical figures
N3934	29 x 23	P	Abraham offering Isaac
NX 18	65 x 52	P	David and Bathsheba
NX 19	51 x 40	P	Three allegorical figures
NX 12	43 x 30	P	Family of Darius before Alexander?
Na 594	26 x 38 x 25	B	The anointing of Saul
NX533	56 x 46	P	Man/woman with lute

Cecil Higgins Art Gallery, Bedford.

Reference	Dimensions	Type	Subject
T18	28 x 25 x 15	B	Esther and Ahasuerus/family arms

Fenton House (National Trust), Hampstead,London

Reference	Dimensions	Type	Subject
*	21 x 17	P	Solomon and Sheba
*	13 x 11 x 7	B	Juno and her peacock/the elements
*	21 x 17	P	Daphne/Narcissus (box panels)

The Fitzwilliam Museum, Cambridge

Reference	Dimensions	Type	Subject
T1.1933	28 x 56	P	Pastoral scene
T16.1939	*	2P	Unfinished/for a box
T11.1945	22 x 25	P	Man and woman in arbours (part)
T22.1945	*	P	Figures/animals/trees
T23.1945	26 x 34	P	Shepherdess
T31.1945	20 x 27	P	Abraham and Eliezer
T32.1945	20 x 27	P	Isaac and Rebecca
T3.1946	20 x 28	C	Vase/leopard/stag
T6.1952	17 x 22	P	Flowers/sprigs, 1669
T5.1954	43 x 60	P	David and Bathsheba, 1700
T15.1928	*	*	Band sampler, 165?

City Museum and Art Gallery, Hanley, Stoke on Trent

Reference	Dimensions	Type	Subject
*	34 x 47	P	Four seasons (reference to Miss Toombs)

Holburne Museum and Craft Study Centre, Bath

Reference	Dimensions	Type	Subject
F227	32 x 42	P	Orpheus charming the animals
F229	43 x 32	P	Jacob's ladder
F236	32 x 40	P	Charles II after battle of Worcester
F238	25 x 35 x 27	B	Country themes

National Museum of Ireland, Dublin

Reference	Dimensions	Type	Subject
367.1887	32 x 25 x 16	B	King receiving gift from queen
498.1890	53 x 42	P	Abraham and Hagar
397.1891	53 x 42	P	King/queen under canopies
73.1907	37 x 12	P	Abraham offering Isaac
74.1907	24 x 13	P	Lady and gentleman in garden
82.1980	25 x 16	P	Man and woman (unfinished box panel)

The Museum of London, London Wall

Reference	Dimensions	Type	Subject
*	38 x 51	M	Charles I and Henrietta Maria.
A21911	*	P	ditto (three/four casket panels)
P49.43/2	*	P	Charles I and Henrietta?
C2371	51 x 40	P	Judith and Holofernes
63.17/4G	51 x 33	P	Adam and Eve (unfinished)
61.199/1	52 x 42	P	Solomon and the Queen of Sheba

C.2373	47 x 37	M	Seated figures

Royal Ontario Museum, Toronto, Canada

932.15	25 x 35	P	Man/woman under canopy
937.15.2	39 x 49	P	Angel with trumpet
961.153.2	43 x 55	P	Pyramus and Thisbe
968.26.74	19 x 39	P	Man and woman with large tulip
968.26.75	15 x 36	P	Woman with vase (panel from a mirror)
982.101.1	36 x 54	P	Man and woman

Shelburne Museum, Shelburne, VT 05482, USA

3.2-23	43 x 35	M	Fleur-de-lis
3.2-27	46 x 56	M	Man and woman
3.2-30	68 x 56	M	Royal figures/heraldic beasts
8.3-1	26 x 24	P	Judgement of Paris
8.3-2	24 x 35	P	The judgement of Solomon
8.3-3	30 x 39	P	Gentlewoman/canopy
8.3-7	19 x 35	P	Olympian gods
8.3-10	17 x 33 x 23	B	The judgement of Solomon
8.3-11	37 x 38	P	Lady and cavalier
8.3-18	*	M	Heraldic beasts
8.3-23	38 x 48	P	Love and mercy
8.3-61	29 x 35	P	King and queen (Lydia Woolcott)
8.3-65	26 x 17 x 26	B	Three figures with animals
8.3-66	44 x 33 x 21	B	Biblical scenes

Sudbury Hall, (National Trust), Derbyshire

*	42 x 34 x 19	B	Religious/court scenes (Hannah Trapham)

Victoria and Albert Museum, London

892.1864	48 x 33	P	Ahasuerus, Haman, Esther
981.1864	30 x 46	P	Flowers/fruit/scrolls
851.1873 A-F	30 x 22	box	P Charles II and Catherine
1070.1873	37 x 32 x 24	B	Ceres and mythological figures
125.1878	37 x 25	P	Abraham, Hagar, and Ishmael
308.1880	28 x 23 x 16	B	Jacob's dream
351.1886	72 x 61	M	Charles II/queen/lady holding snake (wisdom)
745.1891	27 x 21 x 23	B	Sacrifice of Isaac/Solomon stories/King and queen
247.1896	70 x 56	M	Sarah, Isaac, Hagar, Ishmael, Abraham
Cir8.1912	44 x 58	P	The judgement of Paris
C736.1912	58 x 48	M	Raised purl work
T173.1921	7 x 6	Purse	Bunch of grapes
T50.1924	33 x 26	P	Alpheus pursuing Arethusa
T72.1925	45 x 32	P	David and Bathsheba/Nathan
T253.1927	30 x 20	P	ditto/Uriah lying dead
T23.1928	30 x 23 x 16	B	Story of Abraham
604.1928	30 x 16	P	Cavalier and lady (panel for a box)
T142.1931	51 x 42	M	Diana?/Paris/Allegorical figures
T229.1931	50 x 37	P	Scattered motifs/initials, HP 1661
T52.1934	54 x 43	P	Bathsheba, David/death of Uriah. MY 1656.
T117.1936	46 x 35	P	Charles I/frontispiece of *Eikon Basilike*
T125.1937	53 x 42	P	Esther and Ahasuerus
T154.1937	35 x 28 x 18	B	Lady in cartouche
T9.1940	61 x 53	M	Two royal persons
T10.1940	16 x 24 x 26	B	Lady with flower/gentleman with staff
T17.1946	40 x 53	P	King beneath canopy, 1686
Cir14.1947	53 x 44	P	Abraham and Hagar
T30.1948	27 x 20 x 6	B	Raised flowers
T43.1954	33 x 24 x 18	B	Ladies and gentlemen, 1678, EC
T50.1954	51 x 63		P Susannah and the Elders.
T238.1960	52 x 49	C/cover	Frogs/lizards/birds/flowers
T163.1961	19 x 5 x 13	B	Lady in garden (letter case)
T223A.1968	37 x 30 x 20	B	Old Testament themes
T78.1969	35 x 28 x 14	B	Moses in the bulrushes
T45.1973	32 x 40 x 21	B	Ruth and Boaz
T237.1978	42 x 54	P	Esther and Ahasuerus
T44/44A.1954	15 x 8 x 4	Bk	Hagar, Ishmael, Abraham

The Whitworth Art Gallery, Manchester

T8237	30 x 18 x 25	B	Joseph sold by brothers (Hannah Smith's note)
T8829	19 x 25	P/box lid	Female (wisdom)

T24.1984	33 x 45	P	Man and woman, animals, birds, insects

Colonial Williamsburg Foundation, Williamsburg, VA 23185, USA

1955-45/46	21 x 86		Sampler Adam and Eve, 1693
1956-300A/B	39 x 23 x 31	B	Figures representing the seasons
1960-369	*	C	Male and female figures
1962-111	37 x 50	P	Female figure/canopy
1962-112	34 x 44	P	Lady playing lute/continents
G1971-1473	11 x 8 (3)	Bk	Flora and fauna
G1971-1639	41 x 52	P	Esther and Ahasuerus?
G1971-1641	47 x 60	P	Cavalier and lady.
G1971-1643	74 x 68	M	Male/female figures (unfinished)
G1971-1650	20 x 16 x 23	B	Several male and female figures
G1971-1651	16 x 25 x 30	B	Isaac and Rebecca?
G1971-1716	63 x 74	P	Man and woman/elaborate tent

FURTHER READING

ARTHER, LIZ *Embroidery 1600 - 1700 at The Burrell Collection*, London, John Murray, 1995

BECK, THOMASINA *The Embroiderer's Story*, Newton Abbot, David and Charles, 1995

BROOK, XANTHE *Catalogue of Embroideries, The Lady Lever Art Gallery*, Alan Sutton, 1992

HIRST, BARBARA AND ROY *Raised Embroidery, A Practical Guide to Decorative Stumpwork*, London, Merehurst, 1993

SUPPLIERS

Borovicks, 16 Berwick St, London, W1V 4HP; tel. 0171 437 2180; for silk organza and decorative fabrics

Creative Beadcraft Ltd, Denmark Works, Sheepcote Dell Rd, Beamond End, Near Amersham, Bucks., HP7 ORX; tel. 01494 715 606; for spun cotton balls

The Enamel Shop, P O Box 43, London, SE19 2PN; tel. 0181 325 7272; for mica

ETP Sales and Agencies, Goldcroft, Yeovil, Somerset BA21 4DT; tel. 01935 33538; for thin glove leathers

Heathside Crafts, 149 West Heath Road, Farnborough, Hampshire, GU14 8PL; tel. 01252 544 341; for any fine needlelace threads and other textile materials

John Lewis Partnership Stores; for p.v.c. fabrics and decorative fabrics

MacCulloch and Wallis, 25/26 Dering St, London,W1R 0BH; tel. 0171 629 0311; for unbleached calico, vilene and other fabrics

Mulberry Silks, Patricia Wood, 2 Old Rectory Cottage, Malmesbury, Wiltshire, SN16 0PE; tel. 01666 840 881; for 100/3 fine pure silk twisted threads

Shades at Mace and Nairns, 89 Crane St, Salisbury, Wiltshire; tel. 01722 336 903; for general embroidery materials, Madeira machine threads, and silk dyes and fabric paints

Also try the following - modelling shops for balsawood, brass rods and strips; stockists of fly fishing equipment for coloured fine wires (for needlelace edges); suppliers of cake icing materials for icing wire (for hands and arms); building, hardware and DIY shops for thin aluminum sheet, galvanized garden wires, and various glues; Early Learning Centres for white (PVA) children's glue, and timber merchants for medium density fibre board (MDF).

INDEX

ACKNOWLEDGEMENTS

We would like to thank Janet Taff who spent many hours creating needlelace, our niece Anita Donaldson for guidance, all the embroiderers who kindly lent their work, and also Bert and Moyra Campion-Smith, Chloe Percy, Christine Linnell, Barbara Wood, Jack and Tilly Watkinson, Sonya Turner, and Jack and Betty Smith for making items of our work available for photography and inclusion in this book. We also express our thanks to Diana, Bill and Stewart for their expertise in the presentation of this and our first book.

NOTE: all the embroideries and drawings are by the authors unless otherwise stated.